PEOPLE ARE ARSEHOLES

ANNE HUGHES

AH
IGNITE
BOOKS

CONTENT WARNING:
This book contains a very generous sprinkle of swearing. If you are easily offended, perhaps don't read.

ISBN: 978-1-0686495-2-3

First published in 2024 by AH Ignite Books · annehughesignite.co.uk

© 2024, Anne Hughes. The right of the author to be identified as the author of this work has been asserted by her in accordance with the Copyright, Designs and Patents Act 1988. All rights reserved. No part of this publication may be reproduced, stored, or transmitted in any form, or bay any means, electronic, mechanical, or photocopying, recording or otherwise, without the express written permission of the publisher.

A CIP catalogue copy of this book can be found in the British Library.

Edited by Graham Watson.

Typesetting and cover by Simon Whittle · brandstdesign@gmail.com

Dedicated to every single arsehole I've met in my life. You showed me who not to be, and how not to show up in the world.

And you inspired me to create this book in service to society.

Note to the people I love...
Please don't look for yourself in here. You'll probably find you. And we shouldn't fall out over this.

*Honestly though, it's not my fault you were an arsehole.

To my Gingerlings
Garry, Molly, Della, Danny
Thank you for choosing me, saving me, loving me, and encouraging me.
You are my world.

PEOPLE ARE ARSEHOLES
A BOOK IN FIVE PARTS!

CHAPTER		PAGE
PREFACE	SO, WHAT'S IT ALL ABOUT?	xi
	HERE'S HOW IT'S GOING TO GO	xv

SECTION 1	ARSEHOLE TYPES	
CHAPTER 1	WORK ARSEHOLES	1
CHAPTER 2	THE PUBLIC ARE ARSEHOLES	11
CHAPTER 3	FAMILY ARSEHOLES	21
CHAPTER 4	FRIEND ARSEHOLES	29
CHAPTER 5	COVID ARSEHOLES	37
CHAPTER 6	POLITICIAN ARSEHOLES	41
CHAPTER 7	SUPERIOR ARSEHOLES	45
CHAPTER 8	THE WORST ARSEHOLES	49
CHAPTER 9	SOCIAL MEDIA ARSEHOLES	55

SECTION 2	ARSEHOLE THINKING, BEING & DOING	
CHAPTER 10	HINDSIGHT IS AN ARSEHOLE	65
CHAPTER 11	LAZY ARSEHOLES	71
CHAPTER 12	RACIST, XENOPHOBIC & BREXITEER ARSEHOLES	75
CHAPTER 13	INTOLERANT ARSEHOLES	79

SECTION 3	SO, WHO IS THE ARSEHOLE?	
CHAPTER 14	WHO IS THE ARSEHOLE REALLY?	87
CHAPTER 15	MAYBE I'M THE ARSEHOLE!	91

CHAPTER		PAGE

SECTION 4	WHAT ARSEHOLE ZONE ARE YOU IN & WHERE ARE YOU HEADED?	
CHAPTER 16	ARSEHOLE MAPPING: A USEFUL GUIDE	97
CHAPTER 17	ARSEHOLE MAPPING LEVEL 1: ABSOLUTE & AWFUL ARSEHOLES	101
CHAPTER 18	ARSEHOLE MAPPING LEVEL 2: A BIT OF AN ARSEHOLE	105
CHAPTER 19	ARSEHOLE MAPPING LEVEL 3: RARELY AN ARSEHOLE	109
CHAPTER 20	MOVING BETWEEN LEVELS: PLOT YOU & YOUR PEOPLE ON THE MAP!	113

SECTION 5	A CHALLENGE!	
CHAPTER 21	WE'VE COME THIS FAR… …KEEP FAITH IN THE JOURNEY	121
CHAPTER 22	THE CHALLENGE IF YOU CHOOSE TO ACCEPT IT!	133
CHAPTER 23	IF YOU'RE BIG ENOUGH… A TOUGHER CHALLENGE	137
CHAPTER 24	LET'S GET A BIT SCIENTIFIC… THE 'TIPPING POINT'	147
CHAPTER 25	WE COULD CHANGE OUR WORLDS	155

POSTSCRIPT	ARSEHOLES: AN EPILOGUE	159

This book is written with a crystal-clear purpose.
This book is intentionally designed to be...

A PUBLIC SERVICE ANNOUNCEMENT

Definition   *A public service announcement, or PSA, is a message shared with the public that raises awareness about an issue.*

ARSEHOLE | Some Definitions

Oxford Dictionary
   An irritating, or contemptable person.

Cambridge Dictionary
   An offensive word for an unpleasant person.

Macmillan Dictionary
   An impolite word for an annoying person.
   Synonyms – public nuisance, creep or loudmouth.

Urban Dictionary
   A person who believes they are so important that they treat others with indifference or arrogance.

Determining who the 'Arsehole' is within this piece of writing
The *definition** of who is deemed an arsehole as set out within these pages is measured by the standards of the author.
  If your standards differ, you are advised to write your own book about them.
  There is no need to contact the author to inform them of any difference of opinion in this area.

Note from the author
It's published now! Any intention to tell me you disagree is frankly a waste of time – your words will be empty and ignored.
  And yes, I know you might think I'm the arsehole – I don't give a fuck.

***Definition**
        noun.   What is meant by a word, text, concept, or action.

The best place to start...
In gratitude to my wisdom of always taking the right next step... this has been my next right step for over two years. So glad I got quiet enough to hear myself and press on.

SO, WHAT'S IT ALL ABOUT...

Perhaps it was the pandemic, perhaps it was everyone hiding behind masks for so long and not showing their real selves? It's odd how we were when everything was virtual. I'm sure it wasn't just our pyjama bottoms and overflowing sink full of dishes we made sure were out of camera shot. It was undoubtedly much bigger than that. I think that collectively we've probably internalized our crazy for too long. Maybe we even forgot what interacting with people in the real world was like?
No matter how we got here it is where we are.

It's said to me numerous times a week; thought multiple times a day and witnessed every time I turn the news on. We've found ourselves in a post-pandemic, mid economic crisis, xenophobic, intolerant kind of vibe where plain and simple and there for all to see, People are Arseholes!

While I spend a lot of time witnessing it and hearing about it, at some point in my daily pondering of why people behave the way they do I started to think...

"Do they even realise they're arseholes?"

Imagine it... Having so little self-awareness that you behave like an arsehole multiple times a day and don't even realise! I mean we know when we're being an arsehole. I do. Sometimes it can take a few minutes to catch up with me, but I always see it and when I do and can I say sorry to the receiver of my arsehole behaviour, I laugh at or berate myself and take a mental note not to be an arsehole for the rest of my day, week, life if I can manage it!

It's the ones who don't realise it; or worse, do realise it and justify it to themselves! These are the ones that have been my muse.

Great writers and artists so often speak of their inspiration, referring to their muse. Their great source of creativity. The term itself coming from Greek mythology with each of nine goddesses, the daughters of Zeus and Mnemosyne, presiding over the arts and sciences.

A muse was magnificent I believed, and when I felt the presence of mine, I'd know it was the time to sit down and write. That in that precise moment, wisdom and knowledge would flow through my fingers onto the page.

Like most things in life – it didn't turn out like that.

After half a decade of 'writing a book' I knew my muse was pretty good at hiding. I kept trusting it would show up one day, but little did I know it would be sitting in a bar listening to my friend's relay stories of the arseholes of their weeks and laughing mostly with horror and repulsion, that my very own muse would appear to me.

Who knew my muse would be a sphincter? A butthole, tooshie, bum, rear-end or keister?

And when we get past the anus analogies, realising that people being awful would be my inspiration made me laugh a lot too!

There I was trying to inspire the masses, empower the people around me, spread kindness and joy and be the change I wanted to see in the world. Of all the beauty and strength I have witnessed in my life, I'm still pretty aghast that I chose to draw my inspiration from the muddy depths of the most hideous and appalling behaviours.

But as I've already said and will write countless times in these pages – I am where I am. Proof if it was ever needed that I had to pull my head out my own arse and stop looking to the skies for my muse. All that is wise in the world doesn't necessarily appear so on first sight.

This idea was born was in the hours following one of the annual lunches I plan and host on International Women's Day. We'd had a two-year hiatus with the 2020 event taking place in the days just before everything went tonto, when we were still making jokes about investing in hand sanitiser, the looming toilet roll shortage and having no clue what a global lockdown would feel like.

Now we were in March 2022 and finally the world was beginning to open again. I'd saved up a whole lot of banter to share and couldn't wait to be in a room full of some of my favourite people being inspired by great speakers, eating good food, drinking wine, and laughing.

Obviously having saved it up for two years, my chat was gold dust. Being funny, making even the most serious of people crack a smile has been a lifelong endeavour. I love being humorous, shifting the atmosphere, putting people at ease. As the lunch drew to a close, many Proseccos into the day, I was told enough times for it to be uncomfortable that I should be a comedian. My response was that I already had too many jobs, and beside I wasn't really that funny: they'd just been in the house for too long.

Then I realised as I pondered my writing journey, that I've never once been funny in my writing! What is that all about? I quickly deduced that my head was so far up my own ass that when I sat down to write every other time, I'd told myself that I better 'do it right' and not be 'silly'!

So, as I sat with some of the best friends a woman could wish for, I declared that I was writing a book about the fact *People Are Arseholes* and it would be funny as fuck. That I'd self-publish it and maybe on the way I'd find my writing voice. Even if the only people who will read it are my pals, it will make us laugh and will hopefully help me extract my own head from my colon.

And here we are. Less than 1000 words in and already I'm seeing my muse has been all about the ass! Pulling my head out of it and people being it. It's a funny old path we wander…

So, the first and perhaps best lesson of this book needs to be: You never know where inspiration will come from, so look *everywhere*. Even in the shite!

HERE'S HOW IT'S GOING TO GO...

So now you know I'm inspired by my own butt, let me explain what I'm trying to do here with all the ass-shaped inspiration that's entered my awareness and now yours.

Before you begin this book, you need to get onboard with a basic fact of life. You may well disagree with me that it is an actual fact of life, but that will be because your head is you know where.

If you don't agree with this basic fact, then you are wasting your time. Since you've already purchased, I therefore advise that you tear out the pages of the book, attach them to a string and hang them next to your toilet. I chose the option for nice paper in this book with this reason in mind.

The basic fact I need some head nodding on is that...

People are Arseholes!

It can't be some of the people, some of the time. Or I don't know that's true. Or even I'm never one. We need to all get on board with the stated fact before we begin. We are all arseholes sometimes.

For the doubters *(if there are any!)* I will try briefly to convince you.

The arseholes have been in plain view for so long that they now look like normal people doing normal things. You might even have said something like this before: *'Well, he might be an arsehole, but he's not as much of an arsehole as (insert random name of someone whose awful behaviour you now tolerate)!'*
I'm here to forgive you for believing that this kind of thinking is okay. It's not. It's all arsehole behaviour and it all needs to end.

It's like we have been gaslighted as a species! We're so conditioned that we don't even see arsehole behaviour for what it is any more. We reflect that the current arsehole isn't as bad as the last one, or the one over there, or that he could have been a worse arsehole. He was less arseholey than he could have been! I mean OMG! We're getting a bit deluded, people!

We're stuck in a paradigm that needs to be smashed up to fuck. The arseholes need to either stand up and be counted or adapt their behaviour so much that everyone forgets how much of an arsehole they used to be.

So, we find ourselves in a place where I plea to you to only move forward with this book if you are ready to probably see yourself in its pages.

I'm not saying you need to tweet that you've just recognised you're an arsehole, this ain't confession. But if you think it will help then by all means own your truth in whatever way you choose.

The purpose of the book is that when it's recognised and owned, that arsehole behaviour loses its power, and we begin to move forward towards something better.

When arsehole behaviour stops, our life feels better on the inside. The people around us like us more and have better days, and in turn they stop being arseholes too. We all win!

It's like when the police do a knife amnesty, only different and doesn't make any requirement for you to wash your fingerprints off anything, put your maw's gloves on and troop down to the local constabulary.

I don't want your knives. I want your self-realisation!

I ask you to hand in your awful behaviours and see what life feels like on the other side.

So, now we know where everyone is, let's begin. I feel like Davina in the first few series of *Big Brother* just now as I holler:

'Arseholes! I'm coming to get You!'

ANNE HUGHES — PEOPLE ARE ARSEHOLES

SECTION 1

ARSEHOLE TYPES

ANNE HUGHES — PEOPLE ARE ARSEHOLES

CHAPTER 1
WORK ARSEHOLES

Definition
    Working
    adjective.   *Having paid employment.*
    noun.   *The action of doing work.*

Work! That thing we all need to do. If we like it, we're winning at the game of life. If we hate it – well there is loads I could say about moving on, finding something else but basically, if we hate it the chances are it's because it's mobbed with arseholes.

  Work arseholes come in many shapes and sizes and often the arsehole can even be the actual work or 'machinery' we need to use to do our jobs. The machinery can be anything from PCs to diggers to telephones. It might seem like technology has come a long way, but on some days we can all wish the internet would go tonto and that the Luddites had won that day when they started smashing up machinery in the 1800s. But, leaving the machinery alone for a minute, let's contemplate the rich variety of workplace arseholes. They can be split into a few categories:

- Bosses
- Middle Managers
- Colleagues
- Customers

Maybe they all deserve a chapter each but in a bid to rip the plaster off, let's just put them all in the mixing pot that is chapter 1!

Bosses!

Let's face it, we've all known a psychopath boss. One that makes us wonder 'where do these people come from' and say 'What the actual fuck' more than we ever thought possible. Here are some notions that helps us easily identify them:

- They lurk about your social media and use it against you! *Also known as nosey bastards.*
- They have favourites! *See section on arsehole colleagues.*
- They never pitch in.
- They don't seem to know WT actual F they're talking about!
- They don't approve your holidays!
- They believe a complaining customer over you.
- They change the goalposts frequently!
- They make veiled threats that are meaningless and designed to make you scared.
- They swear at you, bully you, emotionally blackmail you and all in all wreak havoc to your mental wellbeing!
- They share their stories of a woe in a bid to win your support or to get you to like them.

- They are liars.
- They gaslight you.
- They think having a break is thanks to their kindness and not a legal requirement.

Middle Managers

We all want to do better and when something's done well someone on the ladder higher up can be excellent because they get what it's like to do the job. The painful bit is of course when they forget where they came from!

- They start bossing you around from the word go.
- They unfriend you on Facebook.
- They say, "It's confidential," when you never even asked them a question.
- They imply a lot of knowledge in an attempt to make you grovel for the info.
- They look at their watch when you arrive at work.
- They start going for breaks with the folk they hated a week ago.
- They refer to 'the company' as if it's their god who must be obeyed.
- They take any negative feelings you have towards your organisation as a personal attack.

Colleagues

Workplaces can be minefields. Are colleagues your actual pals or just work pals? Should you be friends on social media? Do they actually know you, or just the work version of you?

When I look at my life, I can tell you that three of my six best friends came into my life via work. I wouldn't be without them now and they've all been really long friendships, however I've now got a bit of a line when it comes to making friends. People I meet through work certainly do know a 'work Anne' and not the actual me who can often be a bit of a handful. I've made rules in my 40s like never drinking more than 3 or 4 drinks when I'm out with work people. Not inviting them to my home or telling them everything that's going on with me.

Ironically, I don't feel the need to let colleagues get too close because I've already got friends – some of whom I met through work. But it is a definite line for me now. It's just cleaner, as I see it. Here however are some of the main issues with colleagues being arseholes:

- They steal your ideas.
- They go for frequent sneaky fag breaks and ask you, the non-smoker, to cover.
- They tell the boss every terrible thing you say about them and leave out the fact they agree with you.
- They talk shite!
- They take credit for work they didn't even do.
- Plain and simple – they tell lies.
- They're right lazy bastards.
- They get friendly with the boss so they can get perks no one else does!
- They're a grass!
- I'm saying it again because it needs to be said – they're lazy bastards!

Customers!

This is a big one because we all have different 'customers' we need to deal with on a daily basis. Whether you work in a shop, the service industry, a call centre, the NHS, the government, a charity, a school or college, we all have someone who stands on the other side of the work we do. Some of us deal with them all day everyday face to face, others more remotely or less frequently. No matter who we are though, there is no doubt that we've all had to deal with an arsehole customer we wish hadn't happened across our path.

From all the jobs I've done I'd probably say that Call Centre Customer Arseholes have been the worse. There is something about not seeing a person and sitting in the comfort of your home on the phone that I reckon can probably turns the nicest people into total terrorists for a call centre worker. It's a harsh job I'm glad to say I haven't had to do for many years, but I do still shiver at the thought of it.

Here's a few at the top of my list of customer arseholes:

- They swear at you!
- They shout at you!
- They imply, or outright tell you, that you are an idiot!
- They make unreasonable demands.
- They want something from you that you can't give them, or even that doesn't exist!
- They. Don't. Understand. The. Words. That. Are. Coming. Out. Of. Your. Mouth.
- They smell bad and invade your personal space.

- They spit when they talk.
- They demand to speak to a manager.
- They shout and ask other customers to get on side with them in harassing you.

I believe this is a list that has no end, and we could add to it all day, every day. It does however lead me to an interesting consideration for you.

You, the reader, are at least two of these people. We've all been a customer. If you've ever worked, you've been a colleague. And undoubtedly some of you are bosses too.

You could be exactly the Arsehole Boss, Colleague or Customer we're speaking of?

Throughout this book I'm encouraging you to write in it, so I'm going to offer you space to do so, and this is where it begins...

My Work Arseholes, by _____

1.

2.

3.

4.

5.

6.

7.

8.

9.

10.

ANNE HUGHES — PEOPLE ARE ARSEHOLES

CHAPTER 2
THE PUBLIC ARE ARSEHOLES

Definition
> **Public**
> *noun.* Ordinary people, especially all the people who are not members of a particular organisation or who do not have any special type of knowledge.

This could have been titled *'The Nodding Head Chapter'* as I know that's what anyone reading this is doing! Especially if you've ever worked with the public. Or spent time with the public. Or basically just gone out in public!

It was like St Valentine was firing a Cupid's arrow through my laptop while I was in the finishing months of this book. Here's what happened on 14 February 2024...

Violence and abuse against UK retail staff rises to 1,300 incidents a day!

BRITISH RETAIL CONSORTIUM says criminals 'being given a free pass', with thefts more than doubling to 16.7m incidents last year. UK shop workers are facing 1,300 incidents of violence and abuse a day and a battle to control "brazen" acts of shoplifting, as pressure mounts on ministers to intervene to protect retail employees.

Retailers saw the number of incidents of racial abuse, sexual harassment, physical assaults and threats with weapons rise 50% last year, while thefts more than doubled to 16.7m incidents, according to the British Retail Consortium, the trade body which represents most major retailers.

The rise in retail crime has coincided with a period of rampant price inflation, with the cost of everyday goods from eggs to baby formula increasing over the past two years at a rate not seen since records began in the 1970s, leaving many families struggling to make ends meet.

The Guardian Online | 14 February 2024

Before I had read this story about the fact that we now know that there are at least 1,300 arseholes in our shops every day, I had been inspired to write this after reading another news story about a couple being attacked while camping in the Highlands.

I get that it happens in cities because, well, cities are full of arseholes.

But what fresh hell is this? When the arseholes are actually travelling to the middle of nowhere to keep their hand in?

And what about in our hospitals and doctors' surgeries – you know with the people who work endlessly to save our lives and make us well again...

Scottish NHS staff face abuse with tens of thousands of incidents

SCOTTISH NHS STAFF are enduring high levels of violence and abuse at work with more than fifty incidents recorded every day for five years.

Across Scotland's 14 territorial health boards, there were almost 100,000 incidents of violence and aggression logged in the last five years. There were slightly under 20,000 incidents of violence and aggression logged in NHS Greater Glasgow and Clyde – the highest in Scotland. The Greater Glasgow figures include health facilities in Renfrewshire, East Renfrewshire, East and West Dunbartonshire and Inverclyde. In Lothian, which includes Edinburgh, there were 19,430 over the five years, and in Lanarkshire, just under 10,000.

Unions state that staffing levels are too low and the law protecting staff doesn't cover enough workers. Matt McLaughlin, Unison head of health, said:

"Physical or verbal violence of NHS staff is simply unacceptable. These statistics confirm what we've been saying in Unison for years now. NHS workers are facing the brunt of violence in the workplace as short staffing, patient frustration and lack of security resources take its toll."

A recent Unison survey of nursing members showed that nurses are continually working in understaffed teams and the majority of nurses (84%) have lost confidence in the official system to report critical incidence – because either it takes too long, or nothing happens.

Some NHS staff are protected by the Emergency Workers Act 2005, but Unison has always said this does not go far enough. These figures suggest that the Scottish government must listen to Unison and take steps to ensure that NHS staff are free from violence in the workplace."

The National newspaper | 22 May 2023

I'd imagine there are very few of us that don't need to interact with our fellow human beings at some point in our week so here's a couple of the top-notch arsehole behaviours I reckon we need to be aware of:

They Park in Disabled Bays!
Because they'll only be a minute. There's no one in it. Their car is expensive and needs extra room.

They Skip Queues!
Just take your turn pal – we're all in some sort of hurry and you think your time is more important than mine. You know nothing about me. So, stick your assumptions up your arse and get in line!

They Give Over-Worked, Low Paid Staff a Hard Time!
Honestly! If I need to stand up for another shop worker, nurse, or bin man I could actually lose the plot! They're doing the best they can, and they don't work for you so get a grip and go take your anger somewhere else!

They Drop the C-Bomb in Public when Sitting Next to You and Your Kid.

Now obvs I love a swear word. When used appropriately I actually don't have any issues with swearing. But there are some words you just shouldn't be saying in public when surrounded by kids.

Twice, yes twice, in the last 6 months I've had to ask diners near me and my kid in a restaurant to stop swearing so much. A guy seated near us in Nando's recently must have said 'cunt' about 27 times in the time it took my daughter to finish her first bottomless drink. He was pretty mortified when I pointed it out, but pal, I shouldn't need to ask you at 2.30pm on a Sunday afternoon and a place that has a lot of kids in it!

When in Enclosed Spaces, their Personal Hygiene is Over-Sharing!

People and their smells and messes. I think we forgot people were scented when we were all on Zoom. But now we're back in the real world we need to take account that other people will sit next to you on the bus or train; they'll get in elevators with you or have lunch next to you; maybe they even sit beside you all day every day!

Wash yourself people! And clean off whatever the fuck that is all over your face!

They Throw their Rubbish on the Street!

You messy arsehole! Pick it up and put it in the bin! Why should I need to walk over it, potentially slip on it or worse – pick it up for you? I bet you're the kind of person who moans about how much of a mess your city is and how the council need to do more about litter!

Getting in Everyone's Way.
Whether it's on the pavement, in a shop, at the bottom of an escalator you people need to familiarise yourself with your surroundings and take appropriate action when you decide to just come to a stop and chat!
One time I saw folk falling on an escalator because someone met their long-lost pal getting ready to join the up escalator! And no, it's not okay that I need to walk on the road because you've decided to take up the whole pavement. Move along people.

Drivers and their Indicators.
Can you just do what you did when you sat your test and flick the lever the right way 30 seconds before you want to turn? You're causing accidents out there, people!

Public Displays of Affection!
Get a room people. There is just no need!

Cross the Road in the Longest Way Possible!
Why can't you just walk across in a straight line? It's odd, annoying, and quite dangerous. And what about the arseholes looking at their phones crossing the road?

Cyclists on Pavements.
The. Cycle. Lane. Is. Right. There. Enough said!

Talking in Quiet Places.
The cinema is a fortune these days and I don't need to hear what some guy said to your pal. Will you either shut up or go for a coffee or something?

Spitting!
You absolute animal! Just stop it!

Mobile Phone Arseholes!
Get off the phone when you're being served in a shop! Don't talk on loudspeaker on the bus, or in café. Don't hold it with one hand while you're pushing a trolly with the other.
Basically, just know when it's time to be on your mobile and when it's really not!

Personal Space Invaders!
You don't need to stand that close to me. We don't know each other, and I can literally hear you breathe.
Step. The. Fuck. Back.

Need a Seat for their Bag!
Nah pal – you only bought one ticket so get your bag on your knee so I can sit the fuck down!

No Door Etiquette.
That just hit me straight in the face you arsehole! Come on people – it's not so hard to just keep your hand there for an extra two seconds until I catch it?

Watching Phones or Tablets Without Earphones.

If you're in your house fill your boots – but please stop assuming we all want to hear what you're watching. My worst example of this recently was on a train from London to Glasgow sitting next to folk sharing a phone, full volume watching a really risqué comedian! Eventually, I just moved seats.

Long, Loud Phone Conversations.

We're not interested – can you not have that call in private? And if you're arguing with someone, you're just pissing me off because I can't hear the other person and so don't know whose side to take!

I Didn't Ask for Your Opinion!

This makes me laugh to be honest – but when I'm holding a dress or top against me I'm forming my own opinion. I don't need yours. I also don't need to know what you don't like in my food shopping or how it once made you sick or indeed if I look like I can walk in those shoes.

My Public Arseholes, by _____

1.

2.

3.

4.

5.

6.

7.

8.

9.

10.

CHAPTER 3
FAMILY ARSEHOLES

Definition
    Family
    noun.   *A family is a group of two or more persons related by birth, marriage or adoption who live together; all such related persons are considered as members of one family. Examples of family members are parents, children, siblings, aunts, uncles, cousins.*

I suppose it really depends on the family. I can put my hand up to having a few family arseholes and, as I consider everyone I've known in my 48 years and their various stories about their families that they've shared, I think I can be pretty confident that we can all put our hands up to having at least one family member arsehole.

    Families and relationships are complicated. There's no doubt about that. It's why we have so many soap operas filling our TV listings I suppose. Some people's worst stories about their families will be small fry to others. Some's biggest fall outs and heartbreaks will be both minor and sensational depending on who they're telling the story to.

Whoever came up with the phrase *'Friends are the family we choose for ourselves,'* didn't get it from nowhere.

I'd imagine whoever said it, and everyone who repeats it, shares it on social media or even cross-stiches and frames it, had a heartbreak drilled deeply into their life story.

I wasn't sure whether I should write this if I'm honest. But in the spirit of authenticity, I'll go first.

Before I start, I can tell you I'm pretty much over it now. These days it mostly makes me feel sorry for them that they couldn't do better in the face of such sadness. And yes, 35 years on I do still see them; we still don't speak; and I'm not entirely sure how I feel about that.

My mum passed away in 1989 after a lengthy dance with leukaemia. *(I never call it a fight. I think saying people are at battle with something as enormous as blood cancer, or any illness, is cruel. And the suggestion that if they die, they lost makes me feel sick. It's like we're blaming them for going to their graves. People need to stop talking about 'fighting' when it comes to people and their illness.)* I was 12 when she got unwell and just turned 14 when she passed.

It was the saddest time of my life. It took several years for me to realise that 1989 in fact had two major traumas for me:

1. My mum died in a way that felt very sudden, when I was full of hope she would get better. She had been poorly for almost two years so to others it maybe didn't feel sudden, but for me it was a complete shock.
2. My extended family acted like total arseholes and left me with a level of confusion and feelings of rejection that it took me until my late 30s to unpack their impact.

You get #1. Losing a parent is hard at any age but so young and at such a pivotal time in your development was just awful. I'm glad that wee girl made it through and got me to where I am – happy, loved, loving and aging.

#2 though – that was a life-altering catastrophe that even now I find difficult to comprehend. At the time it was a major incident kind of event that started slowly like those mental nights when you promised you were just having one drink.

At the beginning it was just a bit quiet, a nothing to see here sort of event that quickly catapulted into a mix of dawning realisation and quickly slid into what the actual fuck is happening here?

I have a massive family. My mum and dad were both from families of ten. And as well as siblings, my parents had dozens of cousins. Add in all their children I couldn't even begin to estimate how big my family is. When it comes to first cousins, I always had the most of anyone I know – it's in the low fifties, I think.

Coupled with this we mostly all lived in the same area, many of us still in Govan where my mum and dad grew up and most of the others in surrounding bits of the south side of Glasgow.

My mum was the oldest and took her position as the matriarch of her family pretty seriously. Despite various fall outs previously, when my mum got unwell, they gathered around us like a protective shield. They were woven into our everyday lives and barely a day or even meal went past without some of them being in our home. While it was a desperately difficult time, we felt supported and loved. I think my mum was probably so grateful for them all. Always here, always helping.

My mum died on 23rd June. By the Glasgow Fayre Fortnight (mid-July) I think the embers of the impending disaster had sparked. Our once-busy house fell silent as they halted their presence with what felt like almost immediate effect after the funeral.

They just vanished from our lives. At first it could be explained away as giving us time to grieve. But in reality, it was like Mary wasn't the only one who died that sunny June Friday at the very end of the school term.

At first it was a lack of presence in our home by them, and it swiftly became crossing roads to avoid us. Having aunts and uncles walk past me in the street in the weeks and months after losing my mum was one of the biggest tragedies of my life. That blessing of having so many so near, quickly became more of a curse. They broke my heart every time and given our location it was like a dagger stabbing me with what felt like clockwork precision.

I'd lost my mum and now I'd lost many of my aunts and uncles. The disappearance of some of my cousins probably caused the most pain. I thought I was doing my whole life with these people. Turned out to be just over a decade. I couldn't believe it. I was bereft.

I've spent a lot of navel gazing hours contemplating what the narrative was for those who had disappeared into the shadows. Did they get together to plan shunning us in unison? And what was the narrative for my cousins? Did they never ask to come see me? Were they told, no? Did they question it the way I'm pretty sure I would have if tables were turned? I'll never know now, and maybe that's okay. Maybe I don't need to know.

As awful as this was, I know I'm not alone. I know people have worse tales to tell. I am really lucky to say that the important people stayed, and I have never one day in my life felt alone, unsupported or unloved. So, while this was absolute shite, it surely played a part in forming who I am, and for that I am grateful. Because I like who I am.

Note from the author: I fully appreciate that this may not be how others saw these events at the time. They are however my honest reflection on the period and therefore are very true for me. I make no apology for speaking my truth on these pages. It has been a liberating, empowering and tearful process.

So, whether your family arseholes are worse or better here is a list of some Family Arseholes for us to reflect on as we continue our journey:

- They think you don't understand the world.
- They say whatever they think, even when it's wildly inappropriate.
- They assume rights over you they don't have.
- They start an argument with you but get upset when you argue back.
- They believe you owe them something because they looked after you as a child – like it was a barter thing and your dues are up.
- They embarrass you because they can, and they know where you to hit you where it'll cause most damage.

- They claim to not understand you, even though you've been showing them who you are your entire life.
- They re-write history and gaslight you over stuff you know to be true.
- They are abusive because they're family and *'they can be'.*
- They have an expectation you should drop everything for them when they call even though they don't provide the same support for you.
- They bring up stuff that you said decades ago and even though you've apologised 1,736 times they're still offended!
- They have the expectation you should always be on their side, even when they are wrong.
- They ignore you.
- They feel entitled to your time and stuff.
- They talk shit about you.
- They lie to you.
- They abuse you.
- They don't love you the way you love them.
- They don't respect the trust that you've given them.

There's a really good chance that you know family arseholes I never captured here. So now you've seen my list, and since there is no expectation that you'll agree with all my thoughts, it's time to write your own...

My Family Arseholes, by _____

1.

2.

3.

4.

5.

6.

7.

8.

9.

10.

ANNE HUGHES — PEOPLE ARE ARSEHOLES

CHAPTER 4
FRIEND ARSEHOLES

Definition
> **Friends**
> *noun.   A person who has a strong liking for and trust in another*

There's a saying that friends are the family we choose for ourselves. It's therefore sometimes mystifying that even when we hand pick our people – they can still be such arseholes often playing the role of the villain in our lives.

Life has been really kind to me with friendships. I've always found it quite easy to make friends, but with that ease there comes an awful lot of naivety!

No matter how many times I remind myself that I shouldn't take people at face value – I so often do. I believe them when they tell me who they are. I don't question if they're painting an unrealistic picture of themselves – I just take it all in and make a new pal.

Obviously, this has caught me out quite a few times, so I came up with a work around. As awful as it sounds, I have different grades of friends:

My Real Friends

There are only 7 of these and combined I've known them for 162 years. I really do know these people aren't arseholes and if they ever have questionable behaviour, I will always forgive them for it!

They also give me the strength I need to do things like write this book – because I know even if no one else likes it, these angels will cheer for me, and encourage me.

My Long Time Friends

The ones I've known for a lifetime. We don't always see each other; a text is all they get on their birthday and when we do meet up from time to time it always feels like we've picked up exactly where we left off. They might be arseholes sometimes, but they're not in my life often enough for me to witness it. And when they tell me the tales of their life it's from their viewpoint and I can easily get on board with calling the other side an arsehole. Granted, I don't dig deep into the story, know the other person, or particularly care. But we all need a bit of solidarity sometimes and since I never sit on the proverbial fence, I'm happy to get on board and despise my long-time friends' enemies with them.

The Govan Pals

These are the ones I've known forever. Loads of them will probably be reading this book and laughing. They'll have bought the book because 'Big Anne' wrote it.

I can be any Anne with these folk. If I'm a laugh they'll tell me. If I'm an arsehole, they'll tell me. We could go a hundred years without seeing each other and if we bump into one another on a night out, or in any random location around the globe, we'll be delighted to see each other; have each other's back and mostly agree on a lot of stuff – because we were all forged in the same fire.

Work Friends
Well we've covered this. Some are arseholes, some aren't. But they aren't in my inner circle so I'm mostly unaffected by it.

Pals
I've got a phrase I use too often when describing people that is "A pal of mine..." These are people I know and like. We don't text and I don't even know their age let alone their birthday. But when we do see each other it's great to catch up. We're friends on Facebook and bump into each other at events. We like each other's posts on socials and feel as if we know each other a bit, we do recognise though that it's not real friendship. We're just on the same path, in the same city, have the same career – so something external links us in some way.

This category of 'friend' is the one that can change most! They move about the category of Friends...

- They can move up to being a Real Friend
- They become Long Time Friends
- You might have worked together at some point and that's how you met so they linger between Work Friend and Pal.
- They need to be moved along altogether!

The exception is of course the Govan Pals – no one else can join that group. They'll just stay in the same place forever. Really close to my heart.

And this is where the arsehole behaviour is – it's everywhere! Some of it you can be okay with it and some of it you 100% can't be. The reality is that we all have a line so regardless of category, if they need to be moved along then that's what's got to happen.

As you get older, I believe your circle becomes a dot. Often, I also rationalise that your circle becomes, well a smaller circle. One that's slightly more exclusive.

Here's some examples of Arsehole Behaviour that moves people to the outer reaches of my friendship galaxy:

• I find out they vote Tory. This is the one strike and you're out rule for me!
• They moan, all the time. It begins to feel like you've become a dustbin for their shit thoughts and experiences, and they aren't done until they deposit every single one in your mind. You're left exhausted and they leave feeling so much better because they just took a big shite in your psyche! *'You're such a good listener,'* you'll hear them say as they leave you in their metaphorical gutter.
• The say mean things about you.
• They spend time with people that talk shit about you.
• They are misogynistic arseholes.
• They are sexist, or racist or any other 'ist' that you can't abide!

- They give you the silent treatment – as if they've assumed the right to punish you like a child and banish you for a while.
- They attack some of your biggest character traits – the ones they previously applauded.
- They make plans without you and then invite you the day before as an afterthought.
- They post memes on social media that you reckon are probably passive aggressively aimed at you.
- They're offended when you grow and mature – like change isn't allowed.
- They gaslight you by dismissing all of the above and claiming you're imagining it.
- The shit talk about your other friends and expect you to be okay with it.
- They get pissed off at you because your life is going well.
- They say things like, *'It's okay for you,'* as if working hard at being who you are always comes naturally.

So, while I fully acknowledge that on final read through, I am the arsehole for even 'grading' my friends, I hope I've explained what I mean when it comes to friendship. Some folks you'll forgive an awful lot of, others you'll ditch very quickly. And I really do think that's okay.

Friendship is one of my greatest blessings and I can't imagine my life without the folk who now stand with me. But I also acknowledge that for better or worse I've lost some really special friends along the way. Maybe in those situations I was the arsehole, maybe they were. Either way we shared good times, and I wouldn't swap that for the world.

The point is that if we stand by while our friends are arseholes and do nothing, say nothing, then we become arseholes by association. And an arsehole by association is just as bad sadly.

I once witnessed someone who claimed to be a great socialist and fighter for the workers and anyone who needed to be advocated for, hold the metaphorical jacket of the guy who was trying to bully me. In my opinion he's worse – because not only is he an arsehole. He's also full of shite!

I'm not saying fall out with them on the spot. I'm encouraging you to question their behaviour. Maybe no one ever has and just maybe you'll be saving those at their mercy if you tell them they're a bit of an arsehole.

So now you've seen my list, and since there is no expectation that you'll agree with all my red flags, it's time to write your own. But before you do that, I encourage you to identify who your real friends are. The ones you depend on, and who depend on you. The ones who stand up for you in rooms you aren't in...

_____

_____

_____

_____

_____

_____

_____

_____

Finally, when contemplating our friends, I encourage to think about the kind of behaviours you will no longer accept as okay. Whether for you it means cutting people out altogether or telling them it's not okay – getting clear on what you'll tolerate and what you won't I believe will make life simpler. It could even make it quite beautiful...

My Friends' Arsehole Behaviours, by _____

1.

2.

3.

4.

5.

6.

7.

8.

9.

10.

CHAPTER 5
COVID ARSEHOLES

Definition
    Covid-19
    noun. *An infectious disease caused by a coronavirus (= a type of virus), that usually causes fever, tiredness, a cough, and changes to the senses of smell and taste, and can lead to breathing problem and severe illness in some people.*

The last few years introduced us all to a whole new level of Arseholery! Who would even have believed that the whole world could stop the way it did and that our lives could change so dramatically?

  To be upfront from the outset, so you get the perspective I'm coming from I want to set out my stall:

- I believe Covid is real.
- I gratefully received all my vaccines.
- I abided (mostly) by the rules.
- I always wore a facemask because I could still breathe.

- I got absolutely raging with Covid deniers on many occasions.
- I tried not to be in the company of vaccine refusers.

Being in the line of work I am where I'm well known as having a big mouth and opinion on everything, I was invited onto radio and TV quite a few times to talk about it all. My most concise line on it all is this.

Thousands of people were dying of Covid in my city and country. It was my duty as a member of society to follow the guidelines and get vaccinated. Not just for me, but for everyone.

And when asked about my kids being vaccinated and the notion, they could ask why they had to be vaccinated, my response was solid:

They are getting vaccinated and if they asked me why, I'll tell them it's not about them. It's about us living in a society where we do what is right for everyone, not just ourselves.

If your line on Covid is different, you're one of the arseholes I'm getting ready to write about. But at least now we know where everyone stands.

So, since I apparently love a list, here's one of some Covid arseholes:

- Not wearing masks in public.
- Coughing in public.
- Touching stuff.
- Getting in your space.
- Having parties.

- Getting your hairdresser to come to a tent in your garden while the rest of us looked like we'd been dragged through a bush backwards.
- Going out in public even when you had tested positive for Covid.
- Demonstrating against Covid. *Covid couldn't hear you.*
- Encouraging people to inject bleach to get rid of it. *Imbecile yank!*
- You're sure you had Covid in January or February before the lock down and you tell everyone. Many times.
- You had the same disagreement about the vaccine with people like me who advocated for it, 473 times! You were never changing our minds with all your internet knowledge.
- You were smug when people died after a reaction to the vaccine.
- You fell out with those who took the vaccine because you wanted everyone in your life to do things your way.
- You paid some poor desperate bastard to go get the vaccine for you, so you had the documents you needed for that lads weekend in Magaluf.
- Six feet is marked clearly all over the world pal! Will you back the fuck up?
- You post the needle and vaccine emoji's on posts sharing peoples deaths. It's just so shameful!

Thankfully, by the time of publishing Covid is beginning to feel like a distant memory. But it's still an interesting way to reflect on those arseholes in our life, who during this time became even more unbearable. Except of course for the unvaccinated who are the only ones I know still hammering on about it. We know you think you're right and we're all idiots and we'll die! Get some new patter pal!

Let's all hope we never see such times again. But if we did, what would you do differently?

My Top Lessons of Arsehole Behaviour from a Global Pandemic

1.

2.

3.

4.

5.

6.

7.

8.

9.

10.

CHAPTER 6
POLITICIAN ARSEHOLES

Definition
> **Politician**
> *noun.*　　*A member of a government or law-making institution.*

Everyone is nodding in agreement to this one!

I'm very political and always have been. But as the years have gone on, I have to admit that I'm beaten down by their rhetoric.

I reflect if this was their plan all along – to make everyone so angry and disillusioned that we stop paying attention and they can do whatever the fuck they want!

Given the time it has taken me to get this book written I reckon this might be the chapter I was waiting on! UK politics has delivered so much bullshit and arsehole behaviour to us on an almost hourly basis that I wouldn't have believed it was possible.

I will say from the outset that I don't really engage with Westminster politics because it depresses me to my soul. Although I do keep up to date with the shameful bastards

there and spend inordinate amounts of time in complete shock that these fuckers are getting away with so much.
Scottish Politics has sadly now gone much the same way for me.

It seems that part of the test the politicians all did at school about what job best suited them also included things like, having little to no integrity; back stabbing; getting jobs for their pals; self-serving; making a quick buck off the back of dodgy deals; being wholly inadequate for public office; having several jobs so never committing wholly to the one you told your constituents you would wholly commit to; being a liar.

The list is probably endless and could start to bleed into our ever-present list so let's get moving. Before I do begin though, I want to clarify that this is not my opinion on all politicians. I believe, and have known, some outstanding Politians who clearly want to serve their country and people and will always strive to do their best with the highest level of integrity.

This list is of the traits that make *some* politicians total arseholes:

- All Tories – bunch of self-serving bastards.
- They don't do their fucking job.
- They tell lies and when they get caught out don't even resign.
- They bully the civil servants. (Remember the boss arseholes?)
- They expect different rules to apply to them.
- They try to bamboozle us with their words.

- They never answer the question they were asked.
- They preside over chaos.
- They leave so many parts of the puzzle lost.
- They give jobs to their equally inadequate pals.
- They want to send desperate people to Rwanda.
- They want to let desperate people drown in the channel.
- They actually believe that folk living on benefits have it all.
- They destroy our NHS ultimately for their own ends.
- They're corrupt.
- They have no time or desire to understand those who are not like them.
- They have affairs and then parade their poor broken families in front of the camera by way of penance.
- They quote Margaret Thatcher like she was a great leader.
- They didn't follow Covid rules because they believed they were above them.
- They don't resign when its blatantly clear that they should.
- They're just full of shite.

I know I'll have missed loads in this section, so here's your list. Fill your boots...

Best examples of Arsehole Politicians...

1.

2.

3.

4.

5.

6.

7.

8.

9.

10.

CHAPTER 7
SUPERIOR ARSEHOLES

Definition
    Superior
        adjective.   *Better than average or better than other people or things of the same type.*

The title of this chapter almost caused a punch up in my circle! (Not really.)

It started, I must admit, as 'Middle Class Arseholes' until I had an enthusiastic conversation with one of my best pals about it. He rightly said:

'This doesn't apply to an entire section of society. You get working class arseholes too Anne!'

He was right and I would have been an arsehole to believe I could tarnish a whole section of society.

I realised, it's maybe not people's middle class status that grates me so much, but rather an air of entitlement that comes with some folk – who in my experience have mostly been very middle class.

That superiority complex that allows them to believe stuff that really fucks me off.

And just maybe I've picked that up mostly from those I decided were middle class. It wasn't fair, and I was the arsehole. I'm not even going to get started on those who don't even believe in the class structure. I get you don't think it's a thing – I wholeheartedly disagree! In fairness though, I'm confident all sections of society can behave like this. Whatever strata of society you see yourself in, here is the shite I'm talking about, from a very Annie-centric viewpoint:

- When they comment on my 'confidence' as if it's a slur, instead of just telling me they find me too opinionated, too confident, too loud. Too whatever they don't like about people.
- When they pretend, they don't understand me. *(I feel it must be some game of pretence because we're both speaking English and I have slowed down for you!)*
- After they've pretended not to understand me, so I've had to literally spell my words out and am on the verge of a game of charades, they take my word and change it to a more palatable word for them. Most recently they took my *'mental,'* changed it to *'busy'* and gave me a smug nod like I should be grateful.
- When they call me *'aggressive'* because I'm obviously the first arsehole they've met who says what she means and means what she says.
- When they ask me to repeat what I've said one to many times, so I just walk away.

And a few anecdotal incidents I've heard:

- When they assume you're the waiting staff because you happen to be pouring yourself a coffee.
- When they tell waiting staff to round up the bill of £97.52 to £100 and expect a thanks.
- When they say things like, *'Why don't they just buy food for their kids?'* when discussing food poverty.
- When they demonise the poor as if they brought it on themselves and they've never known a moments poverty in their lives.
- When they begin to sell items that cost them £798 for £50 on Facebook Marketplace – just give it the fuck away. Or at least don't harp on about how much you paid for it.
- When they wonder why everyone can't shop in Whole Foods! Everyone doesn't have the luxury of making 'more sustainable' decisions.
- When they judge people for letting their kids eat frozen or processed food! Again, not everyone has your privileges arsehole!
- When they judge those with addictions as if it's a choice. It's never a choice. Some people's trauma runs so deep, that compassion would be a far better way to relate than judgement.
- When they believe that once imprisoned people should lose all human rights! Fuck off you arseholes – they have no liberty so eating gruel and sleeping top to toe isn't really acceptable in a civilised society!

I have one example of complete arsehole behaviour that I wasn't sure where to place in this book. I decided it had to be here:

Grass Folk to the Benefits Agency Arseholes!
This one is screaming to be included for me. Not everyone will perhaps get the cultural reference point of this, but in the circles I grew up in, it's one of the worst things a person could do.

The most damaged in these cases, I believe, are usually children, which is why it could literally make my blood boil. Yes, the media like to tell us all about the exceptionally rare case of someone having a house in the sun and a BMW because of their benefits scam but, even if true, it's something that hardly ever happens.

I say children are the victims here because mostly it's mums on benefits who have a cash in hand job cleaning someone's house. Or watching someone's kids. They make a pittance, because as we know when the middle class don't want to demonise the poor, they love to exploit them. The reason they got the 'cash in hand job' in the first place is because the person paying didn't want to abide by the rules governing employment ie. more cash and actual rights! And the reason they need it – because the state, and wider society by the looks of it, has become okay with people living in absolute, life diminishing, hunger inducing, poverty.

There are a lot of arseholes in these cases, but I'll tell you who aren't. The mums scrubbing strangers' toilets, or the kids going to bed hungry.

The reason these folk are Sinister Arseholes is because I don't understand what's in it for them. I don't understand the motivation for doing it or any pleasure derived from it. It's just plain mean. It's probably a power game for them. They do it because they can. Absolute Arseholes.

CHAPTER 8
THE WORST ARSEHOLES!

Definition
    Worst.
        adjective.   *Superlative of bad: of the lowest quality, or the most unpleasant, difficult, or severe.*

This one is awful but easy! In my opinion those who fall into this group are in fact the worse arseholes of all!

Sadly, most of us have known a few of this type. If we're lucky it's not too many, because when we recognised the first one, they put us on our guard for the rest of our lives!

Their level of utter arsehole-ness made us shudder so deeply that we refused to ever be fooled by their type again.

They walk among us every day. Sit beside us on the train, send us connection requests on social media. They are in line at the supermarket, colleagues in work. In the worst cases they lie next to us in bed or stand shoulder to shoulder with us in family photos.

This particular brand of arsehole can take years to be discovered. Often, they're only recognised by the few in an *Emperor's New Clothes*-type manner. So many of us won't believe that it's true, will deny it and have evidence to back up the belief.

Once I tell you about the Worst Arsehole, you'll fall into one of two groups:

1. 100% YES Annie! You've hit the nail on the fucking head!
2. I don't think I know anyone like that. Let me ponder my life and consider who it could be.

I don't think anyone is getting out of here alive *('here' being life)* without encountering one of these absolutely awful human beings. But I consider I could be wrong and wait with bated breath for someone to tell me on their dying day that they were lucky enough to do life without ever encountering them.

In honesty, if you are on your death bed, I'll leave you with the belief of it. But I'll know it was that you just never saw them because you were too good a person to believe that it's true. That people could be such rank rotten bastards.

The worst arseholes of all are those folk who really believe that they are good people, when in fact they are total terrorists wreaking havoc in the lives of those they set their eyes on.

Hear me again – they act like really good people. Maybe even look like a good human being, literally feeding the poor and donating a kidney. But! They are bad bastards to those they decide are their enemy.

Often the enemy is someone who saw a tiny glimpse of their Arseholeness. And as soon as the Worst Arsehole saw that slight look of realisation on their face the plot to nuke them was set into motion!

It's time for some examples so you can start to paint a picture of these total hell monsters in your mind's eye, so here goes:

- The men who stand in church on a Sunday but batter fuck out of their wives and children behind closed doors.
- The once great bosses who prey on employees when they're down, forcing them to leave their job or have a nervous breakdown.
- Those who claim to be the head of the perfect family when they are in fact terrorising those they claim to treasure with control, intolerance and gaslighting their every thought.
- The absolute bastards who do not expose those who abuse others – because it's not their place. Shameful.

To be clear – if you know about unchallenged abuse you have a duty to do something. Those yet to be abused need to be protected. Yes, it might be shite that you know, and you might not want to deal with it. But tough! You need to!

- Drug dealers. Your business model depends on people's lives falling into chaos – go find a proper job like everyone else and stop preying on desperate people, making desperate decisions in an ill-informed bid to save themselves from their own lives.
- Money lenders. My mother-in-law knew her Provident woman so well, that she was invited to our wedding. Yes, that on was legal, but the folk depending on you are desperate and you profited from their misery by giving them lifelong debt.

When writing this chapter, I started googling what it could be that goes into the makeup of the Worst Arseholes. At first, I was looking at definitions of Personality Disorders. The list gave me plenty to read:

- Borderline Personality Disorder.
- Histrionic Personality Disorder.
- Antisocial Personality Disorder.
- Avoidant Personality Disorder.
- Paranoid Personality Disorder.
- Schizoid Personality Disorder.
- Narcissistic Personality Disorder.

Before I fell headfirst down that rabbit hole, I was feeling like pointing out the dictionary definition of some of these would be good to help us understand and spot them or help them not be such fuckers in the world. But I caught myself first.

I quickly moved to another place. That place is called 'Fuck That Shite'!

The Worst Arseholes don't get to hide behind a medical diagnosis as it if wasn't their fault and they can be dissolved of any responsibility that they were such evil conniving bastards.

They don't get to be forgiven for blowing other people's lives apart with their actions just because they can put a label on it and use their long-utilised skills in lying to convince a doctor and others that they are now healed! That would just give them more power to go commit their evil in more people's lives.

My life has furnished me with a couple of experiences of this and I've heard plenty more which made this list a disgusting delight to put together.

But I also recognise that I won't have captured all the worst arseholes that are out there – so here's the opportunity to jot down some of the ones you've known…

The Worst Arseholes I've Ever Met!

1.

2.

3.

4.

5.

6.

7.

8.

9.

10.

CHAPTER 9
SOCIAL MEDIA ARSEHOLES

Definition
> **Social Media**
> *noun.* *Websites and computer programs that allow people to communicate and share information on the internet using a computer or mobile phone.*

Gawd – where did people put all their crazy before they had the socials? I've got a complicated relationship with social media. Haven't we all? Like when it steals three hours of my day and my phone Screen Time politely tells me I've spent 42% more time on my device than I did on the same day last week!

I turned off my notifications a few years ago and that's made a big difference. Social Media can't demand my attention now. I give it on my terms and when I decide to. This small act of rebellion reminds me continually that I'm in charge.

The biggest problem in that crazy world of social media is of course the trolls. The lay-abouts. The 'no real names given here' folk who have abandoned, if they ever had it, any sense of social decency. They mostly hang about on Twitter – a cesspit of the worst of humanity. Sometimes it grows a topping of good stuff. Random connections, the chance to connect with people you otherwise never would and a source of what's happening in the world and what people are thinking about it.

But mostly it's full of folk who long-ago parted ways with the notion of being kind. The worst lie at both ends of the spectrum, don't they?

US Presidents who eventually get banned for causing an insurrection, all the way down to the guys with no hair, no followers and no idea how to spell. It's the place where incels have found their people. And where hatred is some sort of Hell place currency.

I've had grief on the blue bird quite a few times. It's a consideration when writing this book, that folk who don't like it will begin calling me an arsehole in public a whole lot more. Shouting their empty meaningless words into a cyber wasteland. I split any venom spouted online to me into two categories.

1. They start by telling me I'm an idiot. This is clearly untrue. I'm shite at *University Challenge* and that bizarre *Only Connect* show, but I know a lot about the stuff I know about. Call me idealist and I could get on board, but I'm clearly not a stupid person so you lost me when you started, and I have no interest in what you're saying.
2. They just disagree with me and tell me why. Fine. The world is a place of great contrast and I welcome it into

my life. I'm still not going to engage with you too much, but I like to know there are other opinions out there and welcome the challenge. I'm always up for learning something new, changing my mind, seeing stuff differently, so cheers for pointing a wee arrow that way for me.

And that's where I stop. I don't take it personally because it's not personal. If we know each other, you'll choose a different way to communicate with me. I can't take strangers and their opinions of me seriously. They simply don't matter.

However, I have spoken to folk with profiles that have attracted a world of pain via social media. It's vile and if you do it, you're a total arsehole! You can't be 'right' sitting behind a keyboard when other folk are out there doing actual stuff.

The rule I think we all need to take on this one comes from a yank! Yes – I'm talking about 'The Man in the Arena' by Theodore Roosevelt!

> "It is not the critic who counts; not the man who points out how the strong man stumbles, or where the doer of deeds could have done them better. The credit belongs to the man who is actually in the arena, whose face is marred by dust and sweat and blood; who strives valiantly; who errs, who comes short again and again, because there is no effort without error and shortcoming; but who does actually strive to do the deeds; who knows great enthusiasms, the great devotions; who spends himself in a worthy

cause; who at the best knows in the end the triumph of high achievement, and who at the worst, if he fails, at least fails while daring greatly, so that his place shall never be with those cold and timid souls who neither know victory nor defeat."
Theodore Roosevelt / *Sorbonne, Paris, 23 April 1910*

I'll listen to the folk who are out there doing their thing, saying stuff that they hope can change minds, behaviours, and societies. But if I'm risking being called an arsehole every time anyone ever sees me again in my life, and you're taking a break from your PS5 to throw shite at me on Twitter – quite frankly pal, you can get to fuck.

So, because I've made it a thing here's a list... if you do this shit then pal, I don't know what to tell you. (Actually, yes I do, you arsehole!)

- You abuse strangers for your own amusement.
- You have fake accounts, so no one knows who you are.
- You stalk people you don't even know.
- You change your online name to something that is honestly ridiculous.
- You use a fake profile picture.
- You have multiple accounts.
- You share posts from 'Britain First'.
- You check in at the hospital and then go silent.
- We've seen your dinner! We've seen all your dinners!
- You post news stories that are really old? Did you not check that it's from 2011?
- No, I don't think my 'like' will help save them!

- You share posts from *The Sun*.
- Selfies! Does an adult need to share that many photos of themselves?
- You ask questions that should have been a Google search.
- You ask for 'Recommendations' that should have been a Google search.
- You don't use any punctuation.
- Did you realise that lost dog was in Romania? None of us will see it!
- Posting that you're taking a break from social media. Just take the break!
- So, you have a huge rant and are clearly ragin'... don't be PMing anyone! Just tell us what's happening!!
- We don't care that you're leaving the group... you can simply slip away.
- Dead people can't read FB posts on their birthday. Just saying.
- Your live feed from the concert is shocking! Just enjoy the gig, no one is watching anyway.
- Passive Aggressive posts from work 'pals' on a Friday! Bolt, you absolute rocket!
- Yes, we know you go to the gym every day at 6am, Janice!!!
- Stop with the vagueness – if you're looking for sympathy go find real people who care to give it.
- Enough pet pics already!
- Announcing a 'Facebook Clearout'! I'll get rid of you first, you belter!
- Have a bit of common decency. No one needs to see the 179 pressies you bought your kid for Christmas!

- You're Scottish! Why are you calling yourself 'Mom'?
- Honestly pal – did we need to see another selfie? Did you need to take another one? Is your camera role 99% pics of yourself?
- Aye we get it! You're at the airport, you're boozing at 6am and yes, we know we'll see your feet on a sun lounger soon!
- No Fucks Given memes. Well maybe if more of us gave some fucks...

I'm sure I've missed loads so fill your boots...

The Social Media Arseholes who Rip my Knitting...

1.

2.

3.

4.

5.

6.

7.

8.

9.

10.

ANNE HUGHES — PEOPLE ARE ARSEHOLES

SECTION 2

ARSEHOLE THINKING, BEING & DOING

Definitions
 Thinking
 noun.   *The activity of using your mind to consider something.*

 Being
 noun.   *A person or thing that exists.*

 Doing
 noun.   *Action.*

CHAPTER 10
HINDSIGHT IS AN ARSEHOLE

Definition
> **Hindsight**
> *noun.*   *The ability to understand, after something has happened, what should have been done or what caused the event.*
>
> "I wish I'd done it differently."
> "I wish I'd never met them."
> "I wish I'd stayed in my bed."

These statements, and a whole variety of similar, have been said by everyone at some point in their lives.

Whether it was the wrong meal, marriage, or motor, something at some point has made us wish we'd known before we started, so we hadn't even begun.

The saying that "hindsight is a wonderful thing" has always grated with me so I changed it to "hindsight is an arsehole" years ago. And now, I rarely even do regrets.

It's tough for all of us to own our bad choices; the decisions we made that lead to poor outcomes or the actions that set off awful chains of events. So, it's true – hindsight is not our friend.

But, if we use this arsehole of hindsight, I believe it can help us be less of an arsehole in the bigger picture of our lives.

Recognising we did things wrong is tough, but owning it is even tougher. Most people don't want to take responsibility for their errors. *'It's not my fault,'* we hear them yell. *'I thought it would turn out differently.'*

Yep, we all did. But it didn't, so sadly that means your choice was the game changer. You pulled the flusher on the mountain of shite that just poured down on us.

I think we probably need to just own it and let us move forward.

I urge us all to really reflect on what led you to make that choice, decision or take that course of action. I think if you're really honest with yourself that you probably had a niggling doubt, but something moved you away from it.

Hindsight also gives us the opportunity to question ourselves, and maybe reflect on the arseholes we've let into our lives and minds.

It helps understand that we could have done things differently, so, next time you have a decision to make let the previous ones be your teacher. Make the decision not from your ego, or someone else's encouragement, not for speed or to get on with the next thing.

Next time you come to a crossroad, sit down a while and reflect on the times before when you made decisions too quickly; acted too harshly; and every single time you wished you'd chosen differently.

It's from this place of honest humility that I believe real growth comes. When we have the sense to take time to think about our choices and decisions, we simply make better ones. And in my experience, the more you do this practice the quicker it becomes. I mostly get to that place of clarity really quickly now. Here's some of the questions I run through in my head when I'm deciding how I'll react to whatever is going on:

- Does a decision need to be made?
- Does this decision belong to me?
- What will happen if I don't do/say anything?
- Can I be okay walking away from this decision?
- If I act the way I instinctively want to what will the most likely outcome be?
- Whose advice should I seek?
- Would my words or input help the situation?
- Can I stand in my silence on this one?
- Do I need to stand in my power on this one?

My next move I make is to set a time when I'll make a decision on what I should do next. Whether that's in an hour, a day, a week or a month – once I set the time barrier, I let it float out of my awareness and trust that my inner wisdom is working away on it.

I've found this a much kinder way to navigate my life. And I mean kinder for me. Less pressure, stress and regret.

And in return hindsight has stopped being an arsehole in my life – because I know when I made my choices, that I made them in the very best way I knew how to.

Definition
Inner Wisdom

When I refer to my inner wisdom, I mean that knowing that I have within me. Even when I don't know what to think, I trust that somewhere inside I must know and so I wait for the answer to come up, always trusting that it will. Moving in line with my 'Inner Wisdom' has changed my life and I highly recommend it.

Times Hindsight was an Arsehole in my Life…

1.

2.

3.

4.

5.

6.

7.

8.

9.

10.

CHAPTER 11
LAZY ARSEHOLES

Definition
    Lazy
    adjective.   *Not willing to work or use any effort.*

This is a group we all know and 99% of us have fallen into – if not always, at some point in our lives.

I can admit to being a lazy arsehole quite a lot of the time. But where does it bother us most?

Top of the list I'd say is probably work! We've all been there. When your colleague casts some kind of spell where they know exactly when the boss is coming round the corner and so they snap into sudden action like someone's just found their remote control and pressed all the buttons.

They could also fall into the category of Selfish Arseholes. Do they not realise that the work pretty much needs to be done? So, if they don't do their share, it just leaves much more for everyone else?

The impact causes worse effects in places where there is some sort of physical work needing to be done. Working in retail is the one I think off straight off.

Call Centres not so much because the ruling class has worked out a way to measure the time, we take to do a shite in these places.

They know your every move and that is brutal. So, to be clear I am not condoning this kind of control – more just making lazy bastard colleagues know that they are pissing us all off.

I think the realisation with this one is to actually reflect on our own relationship with being accountable and doing what we said we would do.

It can be brutal in families where one member (usually the mum) can become so worn down by the endless list of things to do that they actual end up silencing their pleas for help. *It's easier to just do it myself,* they decide and stop requesting assistance. So, here's my checklist of accountability for you to ponder:

• When the toilet roll is finished the wee holder does pop out so you can change it, no need to just leave it on top.
• Your dirty washing won't make it to the machine on its own. You know where it is and its really not hard to switch on.
• If there's no food in the cupboard/fridge when you leave in the morning, why do you presume it'll magically appear when you return? Stop at the shops!!
• Leaving rubbish in a bundle by the door isn't the same as actually putting it in the bin.
• You didn't pay the bill, so yes, they will phone you, and no you don't need to be an outraged cheeky bastard to them.
• When they said it was a 'Team Project' that didn't mean you didn't need to do your share! And no, it's not

enough for you to do the feedback on the day and act as if you did all the work yourself.
- Not washing your own dishes in work! Don't even get me started! Who the fuck do you think will do it then Rick, you twat?
- Chopped fruit & vegetables? Really?

Some Right Lazy Arseholes I've Known...

1.

2.

3.

4.

5.

6.

As well as the people you've mentioned above, we also have the opportunity here to reflect on the lazy behaviours you just can't deal with.

So here's another opportunity to write them down, so you hopefully avoid ever doing them.

Lazy Behaviours That Rip My Knitting...

1.

2.

3.

4.

5.

6.

7.

8.

9.

10.

CHAPTER 12
RACIST, XENOPHOBIC & BREXITEER ARSEHOLES

Definitions

Racist
adjective — *Characterised by or showing prejudice, discrimination, or antagonism against a person or people on the basis of their membership of a particular racial or ethnic group, typically one that is a minority or marginalised.*

Xenophobia
noun. — *Fear and hatred of strangers or foreigners or of anything that is strange or foreign.*

Brexiteer
noun. — *Someone who is in favour of the United Kingdom leaving the European Union.*

As a white woman, I know that I'm not qualified to write a chapter on racism, and I really get that. However, in a book about how badly people sometimes behave, I felt it would be remiss to leave out racism in all its forms. Working with different organisations in my day job means I've witnessed a lot of people grapple with our emerging realisation that as a society we're not getting it right. With our white supremacy, micro aggressions, and overt behaviour towards people of colour the time to call ourselves and others to account is long overdue.

I've read a lot on this area. We've all watched a lot because it is ever present. I get that a white person saying, "I'm not racist!" is bullshit and not the attitude that is needed to propel us forward as a society.

So, while I can confirm that I've never been consciously racist, given the society I've always been a part of, and my obvious white privilege, I know I'll have gotten it wrong sometimes. It is only in this place of realisation and reflection that I can set the intention to do better from this point on.

Doing better for me, always means educating myself. So, reading, listening and hopefully learning is the path I'm on with this one. It does seem to me that Britain just now is institutionally racist and xenophobic.

When so many institutions are acknowledging their short comings in this area it seems the light of truth is finally being shone on some shameful practices that should have long ago been called out as unacceptable.

Brexit has proved the shambolic example of how racist bias can fuck stuff up.

It was glaringly obvious to loads of us that Brexit was a mistake from the start.

But people believed the bumbling fools and their bus slogans and thought of themselves and what they deemed had become unpalatable for them.

They didn't want people coming here, taking their jobs and houses. They just didn't realise that 'here' there were too many lazy bastards to do the jobs and so we'd actually be thrown into chaos instead of released from any obligation.

The one that really does get me is that when people not from the UK move here, they are termed 'refugees' or 'immigrants' and yet when British people move anywhere else in the world they are 'ex-pats'. It's such a ridiculous use of terminology that it's laughable.

The question I ask of all the Brexiteers is, did you really not realise that putting that X in the 'leave' box would mean your cousin couldn't live in Spain for as long as they wanted?

That you'd stand in different, longer lines at the airport, or that they'd run out of people to film *A Place in the Sun* with?

Racist, xenophobic idiots thought they could only win. They didn't think with their reading and learning, they thought with their tabloid headlines and sense of superiority, and they fucked it for us all.

This seems like the most obvious of lists to write, but in case you need it, here is some examples of some of the top arsehole behaviours we need to stop and call out when we witness:

- Anyone who starts a sentence with – *'I'm not being racist, but…'*
- Those who use derogatory names for people of colour.
- Using the term 'these people' – fuck off, you cunt!
- Asking people who look remotely non-white where they come from and then questioning even more vociferously when they say Croydon or Edinburgh.
- Telling anyone to go back to where they came from!
- Being offended when you're called out on your micro-aggressions.

The world has changed people. We all go all over the world now and that's a good thing. And even if you don't realise it's a good thing – at least realise it's not changing anytime soon and your opinion on it doesn't matter.

CHAPTER 13
INTOLERANT ARSEHOLES

Definition
    Intolerant
        adjective.   *(of somebody/something) (disapproving) not willing to accept ideas or ways of behaving that are different from your own. Opposite: tolerant.*

I'm declaring this a space to call out the misogynists, homophobes, and transphobes among us! You really are a disappointing bunch of arseholes.

    Misogynistic
        noun.   *Hatred, dislike, or mistrust of women, manifested in various forms such as physical intimidation and abuse, sexual harassment and rape, social shunning and ostracism, etc.: the underlying misogyny in slut-shaming. Historically, witch hunts were an embodiment of the misogyny of the time.*

Homophobic
adjective.   *Homophobic means involving or related to a fear or hatred of gay people.*

Transphobic
adjective.   *Having or showing a dislike of or strong prejudice against transgender people.*

Intolerance in all forms bothers me massively. And I'm not talking lactose or wheat!

Intolerance is a choice and it's one that some people justify making every single day because that's the way they've always thought, and they see no point in changing their minds now.

The confusing bit when we turn to intolerance is the notion that while we should never tolerate intolerance – do we need to tolerate the intolerant person? This winds me up in all sorts of accountability knots quite honestly, but it is an interesting place to start.

Personally, I've decided that the one place I will be intolerant is when it comes to all of the above. I'm alright standing up and saying that if you intimidate, harass and slut shame other women, then you were speaking to us all and you can fuck off.

If you distrust someone based on their sexuality or gender, then you're a cunt and I don't really want to hang out with you.

The world has changed in so many ways. We're all a bit juxtaposed with what to do with the speed the world is moving at, but I see no justification for making others feel small in any area – let alone something as basic as their sex, gender, or sexuality.

As a woman I, like every woman reading this, knows there are spaces and places we can go where we are distrusted unliked by the simple fact we are women. I'm calling you all out men – be honest as you reflect on your attitudes towards women.

One of the most apparent ways we can relate our internalised misogyny as a nation is to reflect on the Gender Pay Gap. Which most of the time we seem to have accepted.

According to the Faucette Society reporting in November 2023, Equal Pay Day in the UK is 22nd November. The day where on average women and men have earned the same wage. The moment when women have effectively stopped being paid in comparison to their male counterparts. The result is that women in the UK get paid on average £6,888 less than men for the same jobs!

I reflect on this very obvious example because it illustrates how entrenched society is in its misogyny. Your actions can't fix it all, but don't be foolish enough to believe that your jokes, banter, opinions, digs aren't having an impact. They very much are and they need to stop.

Homophobia is our next unacceptable issue and one that revolts me. So much so that I am firmly committed to never visiting countries where my gay friends & family would not be welcome. There are 64 countries in the world where it is illegal to be gay! 64!

I can't understand why someone's sexuality has any bearing on anything let alone my opinion of them.

The fact it was also illegal to be homosexual in the UK until in the 1960s I find horrific!

Gratefully I don't know any homophobic arseholes but when I reflect on it, I consider that maybe this particular 'phobia' is rooted in some uncomfortable 'truths' that people have about homosexuality. So, here's some notes that will hopefully help you be less of a cunt in this area:

• You don't need to know about, understand or think about what sex between two men, or two women involves if it's not how you roll.
• Gay men don't fancy all men. No need to be fearful they'll try to 'turn you'.
• Likewise lesbian women don't fancy all women.
• If you have gay friends, it doesn't mean everyone or indeed anyone, will assume you're gay too.
• The HIV crisis and how it was spoken about in the media, etc., was horrific. But let's not believe that HIV and Aids are anything other than a human tragedy. The blame game won't get us out of it.

For me this isn't a conversation about sexuality. It is one of human rights. It's one of acceptance and understanding. It's a place where we can all recognise that we have much more in common than we do that divides us.

The same is also true of our behaviours towards our Trans sisters and brothers.

If I need to have another conversation about the difference between 'sex' and 'gender', I'll lose the plot. Educate yourselves people and stop thinking that a tiny minority of our society are the ones coming for everything you hold sacred!

Transgender people have a life expectancy of 30-35 years of age! This is yet another human tragedy!

My final line on all of these 'phobias' is, to do your fuckin homework! Stop shutting down your own thinking, conversations you're a part of, opportunities to grow, just because you don't know anything about it and you're a bit scared you'll get it wrong.

If you don't do your homework in all these areas, I'm sorry pal – but it's another tick in the topping up of your arsehole's status.

Why have so many people got okay starting off with hate when it comes to their fellow human beings?

While the internet and my own relationship with dairy products has me convinced that food intolerances don't usually go away, this is not the case with the stories of hatred we've been hearing since we were wee and conjure in our own minds.

The next generation give me so much hope in all of the above. They don't appear to judge each other based on their gender, sexuality, or sex. While many of us find it easy to bemoan the young people of today I really do believe we have so much to learn from them when it comes to acceptance.

Intolerances that will Never be Okay with me...

1.

2.

3.

4.

5.

6.

7.

8.

9.

10.

SECTION 3

SO, WHO IS THE ARSEHOLE?

ANNE HUGHES — PEOPLE ARE ARSEHOLES

CHAPTER 14
WHO IS THE ARSEHOLE REALLY?

Definition
    Really
        adverb.   *In fact.*
                      Used to say that something is certain.

Identifying them can sometimes be half the battle. When the word 'arsehole' gets bandied around too much it can become meaningless and lead to the age-old lament *"Everyone is an arsehole,"* or, *"Why do they all find me and mess up my life?".*

Just maybe we need to get better at working out who the arsehole actually is in any given situation.

That way we don't incorrectly tar everyone with the same brush.

Because while I can acknowledge they are everywhere, what I mean is they are in every section of our society, every aspect of our life's.

I don't like to fall down the trap of think everyone is an arsehole – because it might not always be a fair label to put on someone.

If I park on a double yellow line "for a minute" and while I'm in the shop buying my grab-bag of steak McCoy's and a big mint Aero, a traffic warden gives me a ticket – there are quite a few potentials for who the arsehole in this situation is:

1. Me! I parked where I shouldn't have so was basically being an arsehole to every other road user!
2. The person in front of me in the shop who was buying everything from a single loose tomato, toilet roll, a bottle of bleach and a packet of cigars. Have they not heard of a supermarket???
3. Mr Shop Owner who indulged Mrs 'I Don't Go To Asda' by indulging the weary chatter with pleasant responses.
4. The traffic warden who gave me the damn ticket! I mean how could anyone do that for a living?
5. Every other car in the vicinity who parked legally and gave the traffic warden time to get to me!
6. The Traffic Warden's Personal Trainer who encouraged them to walk a 12-minute mile for the good of their heart.

I ask you – how many people in this situation are an arsehole?

Let's try another one. You get home and find that the dog has shit the carpet! Which he's spread up the walls, and along the side of the sofa!
Again, let's see who the arsehole is:

1. The Dog!
2. The neighbour who feeds him every time she sees him!
3. Me. I pressed snooze too many times this morning so never gave him a long enough walk.
4. My son who I suspect gave him left over kebab at 1am when he got in from another night out.
5. My dog walker for putting up their prices so I cut the days I get them.
6. Work mates for arranging the 5pm Drinks Club and making it sound like so much fun I had to go.
7. My partner for being away with work this week.
8. My son (again) for staying late at university to study for his exams.
9. My parents for not offering to travel across the city and take a dog they never got or committed to for a walk.

Again, we could justify that there are quite a few in this situation... but it is perhaps getting less hazy when we look at this way. Because what's become clear to me is, as the old saying goes (but not really) is, *"Some people can be arseholes all the time. Everyone can be an arsehole some of the time, but not everyone can be arseholes all the time."*

Is it the people or the situation? The circumstances or the event? Was it premeditated arsehole action or just how it turned out?

CHAPTER 15
MAYBE I'M THE ARSEHOLE?

Definition
    Self-awareness
    noun.   *Conscious knowledge of one's own character and feelings.*

I've not a doubt in my mind that I'm an arsehole too.

I know that some people will reflect that I was the arsehole in their story. Maybe I was. I like to think my bigger intention could justify it, but I get it didn't always feel like that and so I accept that I'm an arsehole.

There are also folk reading this, seeing themselves, getting a bit pissed off at me for pointing it out and instead of taking a bit of accountability are calling me an arsehole.

I can't ask you to recognise some questionable parts of yourself and not also reflect on them myself.

So, let's have an amnesty as we sit flicking through these pages and let's both decide to own our shit and put our hands up to the parts we know we're guilty of.

Here's where the hand raising for me is…

I know I'm far too much for some people and that there are times when my bold confidence can come across awfully and embarrass others. I know I stand on my soap box too much, that I love the moral high ground too often and that I can be really insensitive if what someone else needs is going to inconvenience me.

I value loyalty a lot which means I can cut people loose much sooner than they perhaps expected.

I love to intimidate Tories, sexists, misogynists, and I'm probably quite cruel in the process of it sometimes. And then I justify it to myself – and as you'll see soon that is a trait of an arsehole. Behaving badly and then making yourself feel quite good about it.

I have family and friends *(past friends)* who I walk past in the street.

I look for opportunities to embarrass someone who has offended or wronged me if I know I'll be in their company. If my higher purpose for being somewhere requires me to make shit decisions, then I'll do it. I get I can keep my eye on the prize at the expense of others.

It's all shite. I shouldn't do it. It makes me an arsehole.

The writing, rewriting, proofreading of this book has helped me get the areas I need to calm the fuck down in.

It's taken a good bit of reflection, telling myself some home truths, and maybe even sending a few apologies out into the world to be able to write this and share it, knowing that I'm not preaching, but rather I'm saying, 'We're all somewhere in this book.'

Strength in numbers being arseholes – no. But strength in numbers looking at themselves and changing their behaviours? That is definitely a club I want to be a part of. In fact, it's a movement I want to begin – and I'm hoping you'll be a part of it.

SECTION 4

WHAT ARSEHOLE ZONE ARE YOU IN & WHERE ARE YOU HEADED?

ANNE HUGHES — PEOPLE ARE ARSEHOLES

CHAPTER 16
ARSEHOLE MAPPING: A USEFUL GUIDE

Definition
    Mapping
        noun.   *The activity or process of making a map.*
                      The activity or process of creating a picture or diagram that represents something.

I'm building up to a helpful visual now. It's meant to let us start to plot ourselves on the Arsehole Map and begin to understand how much of an arsehole we really are! *Don't worry – there are no offending visuals on their way.*

With knowledge comes understanding, and with understanding comes the opportunity for growth.

I get the laughs of saying, *"I'm mapping arseholes,"* or *"I'm growing through my arsehole."*

The humour is intentional, and in case you didn't notice I'm hoping this book is taking you on an *Arsehole Adventure* you didn't know you signed up to when you first opened it.

I stole this idea from something much more serious than what we're doing here.

As soon as I saw it, I knew I could put it to good work in these pages.

A visual for the folk relieved by a page not full of words. A useful guide to point to once this is part of your narrative and you want to point out to someone how much of an arsehole they're being.

I called it Arsehole Mapping for the laughs... maybe it will eventually evolve into something less graphically boaksome! *(Scottish slang meaning vomit or feelings of excessive nausea.)*

As you'll see – I've started in the hell hole of the worst kind of arsehole you can imagine.

As established, we all know at least one. Fuck, maybe you are one! The beginning is the end in this graphic. So hopefully no one actually needs to start at that start. But being close to the end (ie. the right side of the page) is actually a good thing!

If we're starting at the end you're now thinking the end of what? Well maybe it's your humanity, your connection to kindness, your ability to be nice. It's where all the worst ones are, and hopefully where we'll all start to recognise, the area none of us want to fall into, move towards, or have anything to do with.

The ambition I'm hoping to instil in you is that you're always moving away from the start. Or at least I optimistically hope you are!

I hope you'll notice that even when you find yourself slipping back, that a quick glance at this graphic reminds you what you need to do.

That is of course: **'Stop being an arsehole'!**

In the coming pages I'll be encouraging you to get your pen out and do a test on yourself throughout a week to gauge just where you are, but here's a first glance of the arsehole map...

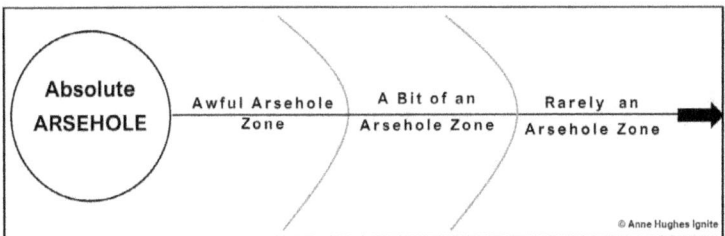

Challenge:
Be really honest with yourself when you look at this graphic. Where you are, and where you want to be will determine if you keep reading or if you call me a cunt and throw the book away!
I hope you make the choice from the very best part of yourself.

CHAPTER 17
ARSEHOLE MAPPING, LEVEL 1: THE ABSOLUTE & AWFUL ARSEHOLES

Definitions

    Absolute

        adjective.   *Very great or to the largest degree possible.*

    Awful

        adjective.   *Extremely bad or unpleasant.*

The Absolute Arsehole Zone

Well, that's everyone we've been discussing since the first page of the book. You know who they are. More importantly I want you to begin to recognise when this could in fact be you! I know, it's a tough journey. You picked up the book and laughed and now I'm asking you to take a good long look in the mirror. I'm the arsehole here and for that I'm… erm… unapologetic!

I'm going to assume that if you're reading this book you're never in the circle (hole) that carries the label 'Absolute Arsehole'. But you know who these people are. They're the scum of the earth.

They gave their pals contracts for work they couldn't carry out, during a global pandemic when the rest of the country had grinded to a halt.

They batter fuck out of their wives and kids and manage to justify it to themselves – or worse, be thoroughly remorseful afterwards. Every. Single. Time.

They use their power to control those weaker than them. They rape. They murder. They start fights and wars. They use violence. They sell drugs. They have not a morsel of compassion for anyone. They are indeed Absolute Arseholes.

I truly hope that you're not in this Zone, and equally that you don't know anyone in this zone. If you do, I'll be honest and say this book is too flippant and you need help that carries guarantees which this book cannot.

Speak to someone about the situation you are in and get help to find your way out.

So much of our society makes me fall to my knees weeping these days, but I do honestly believe that there are good people, doing amazing work that can support people who are leaving harmful situations.

There is a tab on my website which sign posts to organisations you could reach out to for guidance and support. Just check out:
www.annehughesignite.co.uk/support

And if I don't have what you're looking for please use the online enquiry form on the site to send your enquiry confidentially.

We won't reply, but we will action so check back when you can.

The Awful Arsehole Zone
My rationale is that we could potentially all fall into this one sometimes. We'll have witnessed it sadly and we hope never to see it again. These are the sort of behaviours that the perpetrators are so deeply immersed in that they no longer even recognise how awful it is! We like to imagine that if we whisked them back in time to an imagined existence where they were a good person and they saw this that they would be appalled. It's the kind of behaviour that makes us wonder what happened to them to make them so awful. The most compassionate among us may even send them a silent blessing, or a wish for something to change in their miserable life. But the compassionate and wise among us will also know to keep our distance. To cut them out where we can and avoid ever meeting anyone like them again.

Over the page is what the Awful Arsehole Zone could look like…

I deny that I'm an arsehole!

I don't see anything wrong with my arsehole behaviour.

I shut down any confrontations about my behaviours.

Most of my friends are arseholes too so I'm comfortable in my group.

Awful Arsehole Zone

I don't take accountability for my actions or words.

When confronted about my arsehole behaviours I deny them or gaslight others by accusing them of not taking a joke.

I can internally justify everything I do or say.

I have distanced myself from good people or those who call me out on my behaviours.

© Anne Hughes Ignite

Note the blank space on this page for notes, names, whatever you want to doodle! Use it!

CHAPTER 18
ARSEHOLE MAPPING, LEVEL 2: A BIT OF AN ARSEHOLE ZONE

Definition
    Bit
        noun.   *A small piece, or amount of something.*

At this stage the person could really go either way.

If they started as 'Absolute' or 'Awful' this is them on a path of recovery. If they were a good egg and now they are here, it's bad news for us all!

It's also important to recognise at this point that one person's Awful Arsehole could be someone else's Bit of an Arsehole. We all have different experiences of people and of the world. We've all been at the hands of hateful behaviour – it's just some folks hateful behaviour is worlds away from someone else's.

So, if I'm not quite hitting the mark here for you, repopulate the Zones. I encourage you to make this book and this exercise your own. Make this book your own and hopefully make this one wee life we have your own and one that is free from arseholes.

The 'I'm a Bit of an Arsehole' Zone is one for me that we can all probably fall in and out of and we will most certainly be able to think of people in our lives that have these traits.

One that I really wanted to pull out is, *'I'm friends with arseholes and I don't call them out on their behaviours'*!

Have you ever heard the notion that we become like the people we spend time with? If you are hanging around with arseholes, you are really damaging your own perception of what is okay and what's not. Eventually you'll get used to it, and it won't seem so bad. It's like going on holiday and getting used to the time difference, or heat. Within a few days you're there. So, if your best friend of 23 years is an arsehole – I'm sorry to tell you that you probably are too. If your work buddy is awful to others but not you and you've justified that to yourself – you're an arsehole too!

Building the bigger picture of arsehole behaviour could actually be paired up with your family tree, or Facebook friends list eventually. When you put them together it's like you've opened a new door to reality. You've put on 3D film glasses and can all of a sudden see everything so much clearer.

Here's the list that I've plotted but there's space on the page for you to move things around, add to or score out…

To be clear 'A Bit of an Arsehole' doesn't mean they're okay. Their shite (your shite if it's you) still needs to be addressed. The point of the mapping isn't to realise you're not as bad as others – it's to realise you're an arsehole and stop it!

I sometimes regret the way I've
behaved or things I've said.

I always say sorry within a few hours
of being an arsehole.

I quite enjoy witnessing other people
being arseholes.

I'm friends with arseholes & don't call them
out on their actions.

A Bit of an Arsehole Zone

I laugh when I'm reminded of previous
arsehole behaviours.

I'm prepared to be an arsehole if the
'situation demands it'

I tell myself...
*'I do a lot of good in the world, so its okay I'm
an arsehole sometimes'*

© **Anne Hughes Ignite**

CHAPTER 19
ARSEHOLE MAPPING, LEVEL 3: RARELY AN ARSEHOLE ZONE

Definition
> **Rarely**
> *adverb.*   *Not often.*

If you're here, I'm glad. Well done because in a world where there are so many arseholes, you're standing on the high ground, doing life your way, and not letting yourself be affected by all that's going on around you. Because it would be easy not to be wouldn't it, as I've tried to illustrate in these pages.

So, if you are an arsehole reading this you might be thinking how do people do it? A few points:

• Being rarely an arsehole, means you occasionally are. So, this group aren't complete saints.
• Don't assume it's always an easy choice to make.
• Understand that it is a choice!

Remember we all have something called 'free will'!

Definition
   Free Will
   noun. *The ability to decide what to do independently of any outside influence: of your own free will. No one told me to do it – I did it of my own free will.*

Whether we like to admit it or not, it's always a choice. Everything is. Yes, we can blame our family, our upbringing, our circumstances, our trauma, the folk we work with yada yada yada for the choices we make as if we can absolve ourselves of all responsibility. But we do have a choice and the people who are *'rarely an arsehole'* have been making a whole series of good ones. If it's your people who are here – well done on attracting the good ones into your life. **Remember that point I made about us being like the people we spend time with?* If you only know one person here, I want to set you another challenge...

> **Challenge:**
> Take those who are Rarely an Arsehole for a coffee and try to understand how they think and why they make kinder decisions and better choices in life.

The best part about being here and being on the journey of this book is that you'll hopefully now know if you start to slip. Or at least be aware of the choices you are making, if not in the moment at least on reflection. If you make a new pal and they're not here, well that's a choice too isn't it? Give them the book perhaps, but also contemplate pushing them out of your DMs and move on, arsehole free.

I'm sometimes tempted to be an arsehole but then I decide not to.

I'm nice to everyone, even people who can do nothing for me.

I get that my life isn't just about me, so I do stuff that's good for the majority of people in my family/company/community

Rarely an Arsehole Zone

I walk away from Arseholes because life is too short for this kind of shite.

I call Arseholes out on their behaviour.

None of my friends are Arseholes.

I surround myself with good people and wish for everyone that they could attract so much love & kindness into their lives.

© Anne Hughes Ignite

CHAPTER 20
MOVING BETWEEN LEVELS: PLOT YOU & YOUR PEOPLE ON THE MAP!

So now we've chatted through the mapping I encourage you to plot yourself and your people on the map. Work out who is were and if you can put a wee arrow next to their name that reminds you of the direction they're going in. Really important – recognise what direction you are going in!

Now, it's time for brutal self-truth. If you're along the bad end you'll just be calling me an arsehole. Fair enough – I can take it. I hope it's an inner conversation that leads you to realising you are indeed the arsehole. And that's tough. No part of me thinks it's easy realising after years of bullshitting yourself that you're actually a dick! It might make you sick. Gawd, it might even make you more of an arsehole for a while. But I really do believe that something in you will change.

The next time you are an arsehole, you'll know you were an Arsehole. Yes, you'll justify it to yourself, but you'll also know that it was rotten and even when you push any self-recognition thoughts down, they'll bubble back up. You'll need to look in the eyes of the person who really knows the truth of you and how you behave. The one you can't lie to or bullshit. That person is you the next time you look in the mirror, or even take a selfie. You've been unwittingly set off on a path of self-awareness.

Go on – try ignoring what your own eyes are saying to you in that mirror. You might be able to at first – most likely by being an arsehole to yourself. But eventually the truth will out. I sincerely hope it's before the end of your life when you reflect that you got it all wrong and it's too late to get it right now. What if you live that truth out for eternity? I don't think it's worth the risk.

When you slip back an arsehole... let's get honest.

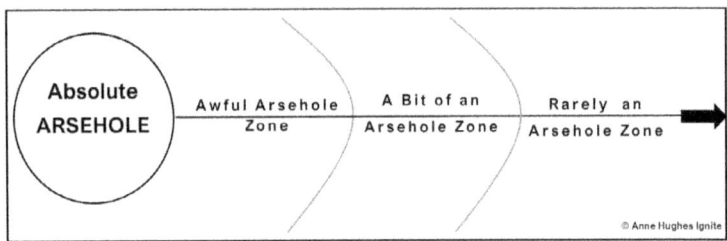

So, here's the reality – the chances of us moving between these levels on a yearly, monthly, weekly, or even hourly basis are probably quite high. Especially in the early days of this journey.

What's needed here is for you to be exceptionally honest with yourself. You're the only one who truly knows where you are here, and even if you're lying to yourself, you know you are so you're just being a right arsehole to yourself too.

So first up, I want you to get honest and over the space of the next week plot yourself on this chart with brutal honesty so you can see how your behaviours are actually showing up in your life...

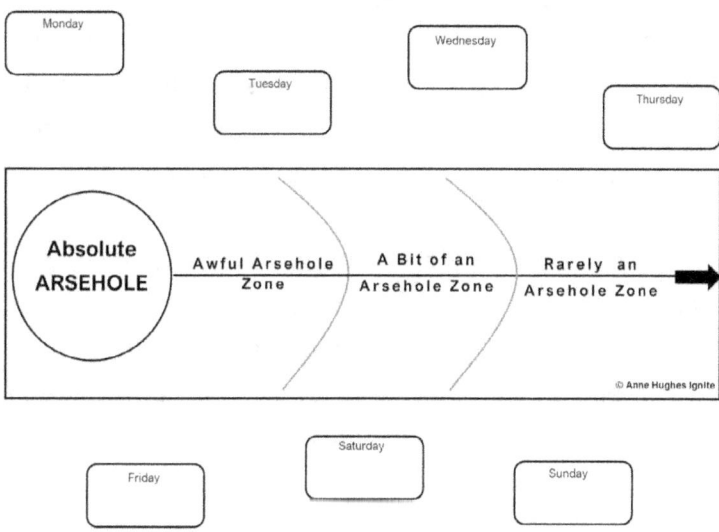

> **Challenge:**
> Honestly draw a line each day of the next week to the area you sat in most of the time, daily.
> For added impact, there is space for you to note the number of arsehole actions you chose to make too!

How did that feel? Maybe you've not done it yet, but you're reflecting on the kind of week you knew you had. It's tough being honest with the man in the mirror, isn't it?

While you're doing this for yourself you might also decide to do it for some of the people you spend most of your time with. Now that's always going to be based on your perception of them and if they did it themselves, they could potentially mark themselves much differently. Which is why the next exercise is just for you, and if you've not done so already, it might be time to keep your book in a private space and not randomly leave it lying around where someone could pick it up, see you think they're an awful arsehole and WW3 breaks out in your life!

In this next image, I'm inviting you to really think about those you spend your time with and how you feel they show up in your life.

This is subjective and the intention is never that you will show it to them and make it some sort of court admissible proof that they are in fact an arsehole.

My intention with this exercise is that you begin to appreciate what behaviours you have:

- Become used to.
- Stopped noticing.
- Now think aren't so bad.

This is really an exercise in self-awareness. One that lets you reflect on how far you've maybe come on the journey of life in what you tolerate and what you could decide to extinguish from your life altogether.

Challenge:
Put the names of the people in your family, workplace, community, friend group or any group in each of the boxes depending on what kind of arsehole they are.

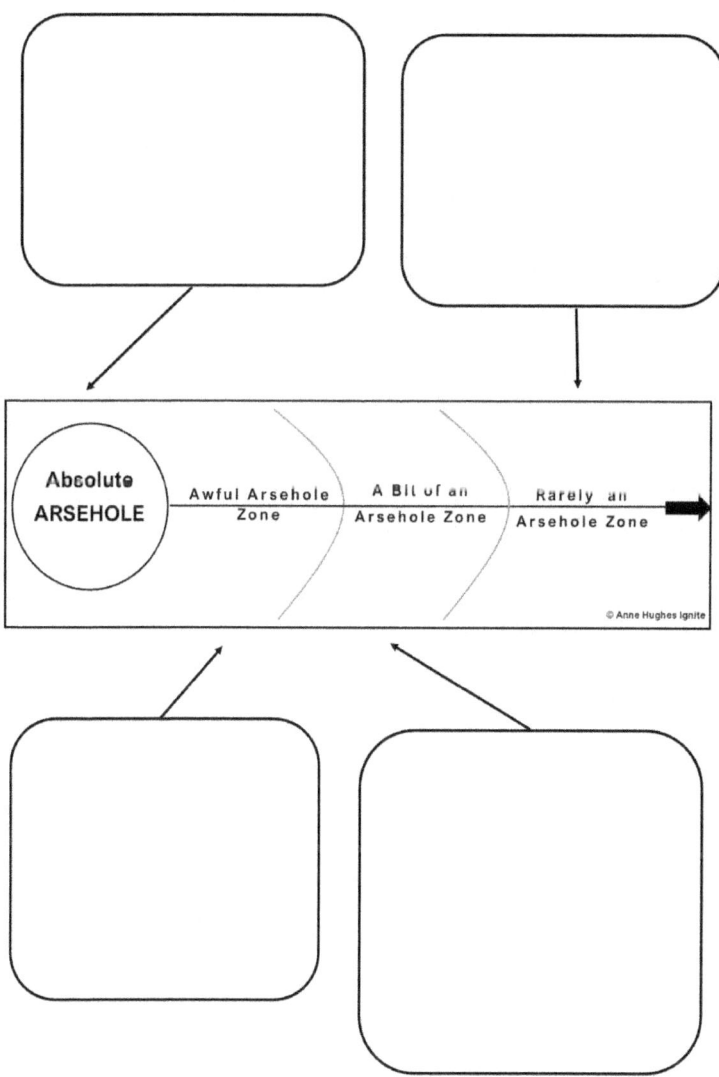

SECTION 5

A CHALLENGE!

ANNE HUGHES — PEOPLE ARE ARSEHOLES

CHAPTER 21
WE'VE COME THIS FAR...
...KEEP FAITH IN THE JOURNEY

So, you've come all the way through this book, nodding, laughing, raging as you read about the arseholes of the world, and we finally get the point! To the crux of the story!

The point of this book was never really to remind you of all the arseholes you have known. It wasn't meant to make you laugh either, although I hope it did a few times.

It defo wasn't meant to make you cry, and if it did, I'm sorry. The arseholes really did get to you.

The point of the cheeky title, all the pages, of me coming up with the idea alone was to get you to recognise that maybe you are the arsehole!

Sorry if you feel you were brought here under false pretences but what can I say! I'm doing it for the worldwide good! I'm doing it for humanity!

I'm imagining you might have gone from laughing, to rage, to realisation and, hopefully not but just maybe, to feeling a bit of shame.

While the purpose of the book is now quite clear – to help people understand where in their lives they are arseholes, I really don't encourage anyone to linger about in shame for too long. It's the worst energy to be in and no good can come from it.

So, if that's where you are let's begin to consider how you could do stuff differently in future. When you know better you do better. So let everything that's gone before this very moment be, and make new, kinder decisions from now on.

Of course, there is another group out there. While they are arseholes and have seen themselves many times in this book, they're still laughing about it and taking delight in the havoc they've caused. If that's you – you're an arsehole. Also, I have a plan that could see you and your type wiped out so watch this space!

*In reality I don't think these people are still reading, tbh.

'When You Know Better You Do Better'

Maya Angelou, one of my favourite teachers, said this frequently enough that it's now seared on my brain.

For those of us committed to doing better there is no point in lingering in the past for too long. We're not going that way. If this is you, I reckon you have two choices:

1. Reflect on the people you may have scorned, look them up and apologise.
2. Reflect on the behaviours that caused upset and firmly commit to never perpetrating them again.

You could of course do both. My issue with #1 is that if those people are now arseholes, they won't get the point of your apology and the intention behind it. They could be such arseholes that they lead you back down that road. So, I am a big advocate of recognising where we went wrong and being determined to move forward differently.

This is where our real power lies.

No one else needs to be involved in our journey of realisation and redemption. It's all an inside job anyway. And I mean everything.

Our lives are all about us. Our thinking creates it, our inner dialogue and feelings feed it and our imagination makes up what everyone else is thinking and doing. I really believe that if we all just took a bit more time on our inner selves that the whole world could change.

I did a lot of online workshops and seminars in the pandemic. It became a bit like my Netflix. I didn't do many box sets, but wow I did a lot of navel-gazing, as my husband calls it. I would attend a workshop, realise something I never thought before and go down the rabbit hole of reflecting on all the events and decisions of my life I could remember and what they might have been about.

The most powerful of them all was the stuff I signed up to with Michael Neill. He really turned my thinking on its head. *(Defo Google him.)*

The most momentous realisation came at some point in late 2020. As I mentioned chapters ago, my mum died when she and I were both too young. This left me with a pretty deep-seated belief that I would also die in my 40s. I didn't worry about it, overthink it, or even verbalise it to anyone. But I believed it the way I believe if I drop my mug of tea on my laptop, it'll be fucked.

Anyway, as I sat there at my desk one dark and drizzly evening in Glasgow it suddenly hit me. It was never true! I made it up, believed it as truth and made it a cornerstone of my being. And it was never true. I was shook!

And the biggest 'Aha!' moment wasn't that I probably won't die in my 40s. It was that if I'd believed that the way I did for so long, what other bullshite have I been carrying around thinking it was truth for my whole life?

So, I now want to reflect it back on you.

What If You're Full of Shite?
- There is a distinct possibility that you are indeed believing things that aren't true about yourself.
- There is a distinct possibility that you are indeed believing things that aren't true about others.
- There is the possibility that you didn't see what you saw, but what you thought you saw.
- There is a good chance that you've made up a lot of stuff about some people in your life.
- There's also a good chance that you believed stuff that someone else made up about people in your life.
- Things might not have happened for the reasons you thought they did.

Yes, you get the idea. There's a lot of stuff that's maybe got muddy in our lives and it led us to what seemed like a logical place, when it is in fact a place where we never needed to go.

And the reason I'm taking you down this path, you wonder...?

It's to help you understand why past arsehole behaviour on your own part could have been a bit misguided.

What I don't encourage you to do is start off on a neverending venture to try to understand why anyone else in your life is an arsehole. As I said, it's an inner journey. It's also their shit to deal with, so leave them to it. And if they never get to this place, well that's just a shame for them. Going through life as an arsehole, despite how much they appear to enjoy it, can't be a good way to do life. I often reflect with some of the arseholes I've known, that they are in my life to show me how not to turn up in the world. They taught me with all their hatefulness, that I never want to be like them. They show me that for sure, and so I grow my internal list of what is unacceptable. Unacceptable for me, for my life and for the people I choose to have in my life.

This leads me straight to something else I really want your thinking to grapple with.

We all get to decide who is in our life and the impact they can have. Yes, I get it. Often it doesn't feel like we have much choice. But that's because we've believed we don't for so damn long. But we do.

Like so much of this stuff I'm chatting about, with behaviours, decisions and thinking – it's like a muscle we need to work to strengthen.

I can tell you hand on heart that I don't have any arseholes in my life.

Have I had arseholes in my life? 100%

Do I know some arseholes? 100%

But, by working this muscle of having a clear definition of what's okay and what's not okay for my world I've managed to silence them and cut them out. I don't ever have any expectation of myself to spend time with people I don't want to. Yes, we might find ourselves in the same place, chatting to the same people. But I don't let them have access to me and my inner being.

I throw up my defences as freely as I used to throw up my kebab after a night out and 10 pints of cider and blackcurrant.

I've also cut people out of my life who crossed over my line. Who have behaved in a way that I just don't want that kind of shit around me.

When you get clearer on what you stand for, you get clearer on where your line is. And once you put it down, mark it in the sand, I encourage you to shimmy back and redraw it for no one! And I mean no one.

Even the people I love most in the world know where my lines are on some stuff. Here's a few of my principles on what is unacceptable:

- Voting Tory.
- Violence in all forms.
- Misogyny.
- Racism.
- Intolerance.
- Hatred of any group. (Except Tories!)
- Bullying behaviour.

I've made it clear to those I hold close over many years that if they vote Tory, they go. If they are cruel to others, they can't spend time with me. If they have intolerance to any group because of faith, sexuality, race that it's a no-no. It might sound like this could be difficult – but it's not. In fact, I would put to you that it makes my life so much simpler.

If I am clear on my line and where it is, and I'm authentic enough to ensure those around me know these things about me then it's simple. Those who are here to stay know exactly who I am, and I know exactly the kind of people that I don't want to waste my time, energy or even if I say so myself, gold-dust banter on. Indeed, I've even been known to turn my back on someone mid conversation if they make a comment or show their truth that crosses my line. It's never confrontational, and while yes, they're probably left a bit confused, I really don't care. Be gone from my life in this instant! And just like magic, they're gone.

Of course – this does mean some people might not like me. Which brings me to one of the best truths I ever came to realise and live:

I Don't Care If You Like Me, I'm Not Here to Make Pals. I've Got Pals.

I appreciate everyone's list will be different. So, don't depend on mine, here's space to write one of your own:

Behaviours and actions that cross my line...

1.

2.

3.

4.

5.

6.

7.

8.

9.

10.

When it comes to my list, I do concede that a bit of brain damage in 2017 (maybe another book of mine you can look up, depending on when you read this) does probably contribute to this for me but it's really liberating so I encourage you to take note and give it a try.

As was recently announced, there are soon going to be 8 billion people on the planet! I mean, I'm not much of an environmentalist, but that is terrifying.

And when we consider how many of them could be arseholes, it's even worse!

I mean look at how many zeros that number even has:

8,000,000,000

Note to self: Keep writing, Annie! We need to start doing something about all the arseholes and their arsehole behaviours!

There is a simple fact I want you first to acknowledge and concede to be true:

'I don't like everyone I know or everyone I meet.'

Why therefore would you expect everyone you know or meet to like you?? It's actually a bit insane.

I mean, if you're a Tory reading this, I'm a bit repulsed I made money off you! But my optimistic, hopeful side also wishes for you that you'll see Tories for the arseholes they are, recognise it was an arsehole move ever voting for them and stop being one. I am that hopeful for you.

By not wanting everyone to like us, we free ourselves to be authentic in the world. And in a world where we're less fake and more real we will naturally find a way to be less of an arsehole. Because we'll not find ourselves in places where we don't need to be. Where we surround ourselves with people who match us in their beliefs, actions, and behaviours. Eventually we find ourselves living an arsehole free existence. Your line in the sand can become so clear that even arseholes you don't know stay away from you. They get the vibe, the sense that you won't put up with their particular brand of arsehole, so invariably they will find an easier target. Poor bastards – if you know these people, give them this book.

Imagine if we can make this happen! All the arseholes could just be left with each other. I hope they all meet their match, realise how fucked up they are and either move to an island together or get a grip and change their ways.

Start Where You Are

I do get that I make it sound easy.

I also get you might think I'm an arsehole for making it sound easy.

And I'm sorry to be the arsehole who is telling you that while it's not necessarily easy at first, it's a bit like going a bike. Once you get it, you get it, and you'll never fall off again.

My advice is to begin where you are. I mean it's the only place we can ever really begin anyway. The insanity of trying to be somewhere we're not is like expecting 8 billion people to like you!

So how do you start?

You must know one arsehole you can cut off, here and now. Maybe start with your social media. People who share posts from Britain First or *The Sun* are always cut off immediately for me.

What's your line? Either cut them off in silence or tell them and all their arsehole pals that you're cutting them off for sharing this kind of shite!

Next – let's look at the work colleagues. If (insert any name) is such an arsehole, why do you still go on your tea break with them? Just stop. Have your tea break with someone else. Hell, I'd rather sit in the toilet and tell them I had explosive diarrhoea than spend 20 minutes with some people! *Top tip: if you ever need an excuse that will get no further enquiry, explosive diarrhoea is the one. No one, and I mean NO ONE wants to find out any more about – or be in the presence of – explosive diarrhoea. (In my experience anyway.)*

The point is, diarrhoea aside, find a way to distance yourself from them. Do you know there are people that don't speak to you because you hang out with that person? That you could have a whole new experience of your work and the people in it if you just stayed the fuck away from the arsehole? You could in fact have become an arsehole by association in other people's lists!

Family is different and it's a tougher cookie to crack. If you married an arsehole, well my sister is a divorce lawyer, so we can fix that one.

If you were born to the same parents as an arsehole, well you might need to see them sometimes, but work hard on those vibes you're giving off and that will take care of itself. They'll either stop being an arsehole, or you'll stop caring that they're an arsehole, so you won't feel the impact of what they say or do.

If you're the parent – well, there's a whole section dedicated to our young people at the end of the book. But if you're children are arseholes – sorry but it might be your fault because they learned it somewhere. Gift them this book and see what happens.

Friends are what they say on the tin. The quotes, gift cards, mugs, keyrings and cross stiches tell us all the time 'friends are the family you chose for yourself'.

You made a bad choice when you picked a pal who was an arsehole. Maybe it was because they tricked you, or maybe it was because you were an arsehole too, so you were a pair of arseholes walking your arsehole paths together. Either way you chose them. By virtue of this fact, you are free to un-choose them too. Get them to fuck out of your life. Block their number, unfriend them on social media, do whatever you need to do to walk in a different direction. In case no one ever told you – you are free to be pals with however you want to be. You're not connected at the hip! This bit can't finish without me stressing to you: be more careful of who you choose to be your friends in future!

CHAPTER 22
YOUR CHALLENGE
IF YOU CHOOSE TO ACCEPT IT!

Definition
> **Challenge**
> *noun.* *(Situation of being faced with) something that needs great mental or physical effort in order to be done successfully, and therefore tests a person's ability.*

This is a whacky place to get to. One that only came to me in those years of procrastination between starting this book and finishing it.

All those behaviours you've recognised you have as you've moved through these pages – I want you to pick the top 5 and I encourage you to bring them to an end now. In this very moment to determine that you will never be that particular brand of arsehole ever again!

Some points that need to be made about arsehole behaviours...

It was <u>your</u> fault you did them.
If you think it was because of the way you were brought up, well the fact you have awareness that you need an excuse means you also have the awareness that it was shite thing to do. It wasn't an automatic response, like crying when you cut an onion. It was a choice. A choice that you made. And it was a shite choice so don't make it again.

The fact you don't like the person you did them to.
Has absolutely fuck all to do with it. You're either an arsehole or you're not. You can't be picky about who you're an arsehole towards – it's not about the person receiving. It's about the person delivering. Just fuck up and stop being an arsehole to everyone.

It wasn't a 'Joke'!
It isn't funny, you fucked up arsehole. No one else is laughing. If you're honest you know it wasn't a joke. You know you were being an arsehole and if you genuinely don't, that just tells you how long you've been an arsehole for doesn't it? If no one else is laughing it wasn't funny.

You can't justify it!
I actually don't care how much of an arsehole the other person may or may not be. This is an inside job remember. Where you never reminded as a kid that you wouldn't jump in the river even if everyone else did?

Changing the folk you're around if you're acting like them is not a justification for it. It's not okay, it is choice, and you are an arsehole for doing it.

How do you start being a non-arsehole?
You just begin. I really urge you to share it with others because that always makes us more accountable, doesn't it? It's like if we do a Zumba class with a pal.

Do what's safe for you though – not everyone is comfortable being vulnerable, especially if they've spent too much time around arseholes. Here's some ideas, or make up your own:

• Write them down and text your commitment to never doing them again to the person you trust most in the world.
• Abbreviate what they mean, write them down and put it somewhere you'll see often.
• Set an alarm on your phone with a specific ring tone for 07:47 every day, and as soon as you hear that noise or tune you are reminded that you are no longer an arsehole.
• Use your abbreviations to make an image and set it as your phone wallpaper.
• Decide on a symbol that will always remind you of the commitment you're making and plot it around your home to remind you every time you see it.
• Tweet and tell me – and everyone else on Twitter.
• Sign up to my mailing list and I'll send you reminder emails when you're least expecting them!

- Get a tattoo! (Bit extreme)
- Get letter magnets and write it on your fridge.
- Post it on your social media for all to see – even the other arseholes. It could go like this:

> "I've realised I'm a bit of an arsehole, so I've decided to stop…"

So, we begin where we are, your first challenge if you choose to accept it…

Here's some space to practice on – committing it to paper is the first step on the journey…

CHAPTER 23
IF YOU'RE BIG ENOUGH: A TOUGHER CHALLENGE

Definition
> **Tougher**
> *adjective.* Strong. Not easily broken or made weaker.

This time I want you to go think about all the arseholes you identified in your life and write a list of who in your circle is a perpetrator of the arsehole behaviours. Now it might be someone you have no power over, and you don't get to decide how much you need to be in their company. I'm taking bosses, teachers, parents. I never said this would be easy, but I do think you have some choices.

The Arseholes in my life...

1.

2.

3.

4.

5.

6.

7.

8.

9.

10.

    Highlight or underline these ones and once you're done sit with it for a while (between an hour and a month) and consider how many people in your life are actually arseholes. I know it's unbelievable. How did you never see it before? How have they possibly been getting away with it this long? And why does it appear that people didn't even notice it and are just unaware of it now?

I know. It can sometimes feel like the world is fucked! But let's keep doing our thing and see if we can make a bit of a dent in it. It's worth a try I reckon.

Write them down – you don't want to forget them...

Behaviours that disgust me...

1.

2.

3.

4.

5.

I do contemplate getting you write them out a hundred times like ole time school punishment style, so you don't forget. But I'd maybe be a bit of an arsehole to insist on that, so you do you and what works best for you.

Whatever you do, do it with passion and commitment. Do it with the passion and commitment of the relentless arseholes you're now thinking about.

So, you've got your list, and with it you've got the known culprits too.

Now for the next challenge... I'm writing it in first person, and I want you to say it out loud as many times as you need to for it to become a pillar of your values. Don't underestimate how important this part of the process is. I need you to mean it and own it...

- *I will never in my life remain silent upon witnessing these behaviours ever again.*
- *I will stand against it every single time.*
- *I will speak out even when I feel uncomfortable doing so.*
- *I will stand against it for people I don't even like.*
- *I will speak against it for strangers.*
- *I will never let this happen in my presence again without voicing my disgust.*
- *I will make this point even when I'm scared to do so.*

I know. It's a lot. Especially if you're not as much of a big mouth as me. But cast your mind back to all the times various arseholes got away with being awful to you and no one said a word. When people sat silently but as soon as the perpetrator left the room jumped to your defence. It fell on the wrong ears and the arsehole never had to answer for their arsehole behaviour.

While you raged with the pain or embarrassment of what had just happened you thought to yourself, *"Aye sure pal – it's good having you on my side when we're the only ones here."*

When you told others about it, they said, *"Did no one say anything?"* and the fact they didn't became almost as embarrassing and humiliating as the event itself.

And so, you slowly became accepting of the bad behaviour, and when it happened to the people who didn't stand up for you, you were ashamed to admit that you actually derived a wee bit of pleasure from it. Because you had escaped it that time and now they knew how it felt. You looked at each other, equally as shamed and broken, neither of you able to stand up to the apparent wielder of the power.

Well, no more!

Look at the date and time my friend because this might just be the moment when it all begins to change!

I should clarify at this point, that I'm not naive enough to think that the arseholes will just sit down and shut up because you call them out. The road ahead may not be an easy one which is why I'm inviting you to try it just one day per week so you can get used to it.

What I can guarantee you though, is that the more you do it, the easier it will get, and every time you do, someone will be so grateful to you. Even if they're too scared to say it. In fact, I think they'll remember you and your bravery in that moment for the rest of their lives.

So, What Will the Arseholes Do Now?

I don't have a definitive answer for this. What I have are some thoughts and some experiences of my own.

In my experience the worst arseholes are actually shitebags. At some point I image folk were pretty big arseholes to them, and no one stood up for them, so they decided it would be easier to just be like them. They rationalised to themselves that the only way they could be better than the bad guys was to be worse than the bad guys. I get it, and I do in fact have some compassion for that experience of the world.

I have so much compassion in fact that my writing this book, and you reading it, I believe we could set a lot of arseholes free from themselves.

Imagine it. There's maybe an arsehole reading this, and until this moment they never realised it all began with someone being evil to them. They never meant to get caught up in a snowball of hatred, but they just did. It was the hand they were delt. At the beginning they knew it was bad news, but they justified it to themselves. They justified it so many times that it became 'normal' behaviour. In the early days they saw themselves in the eyes of the person they had belittled and shamed, but then life rubbed that off and they got to a place where they didn't even question themselves. And do you know what happened next? No one ever called them out on it, so they probably thought it wasn't that bad. It got them the result they wanted, and it was all part of the game of life.

We need to stand up again it to save the victims 100%! But maybe on the way we'll save a few of the arseholes too.

Top Tips for Dealing with an Arsehole
Walk Away! Walk Away! Walk Away!

I honestly think the safest way to deal with some folk is to take away their audience. Every day we show people how to treat us. It might not feel like it, but it's true. Laughing at sexist or racist jokes for example, shows others you're on their humour wavelength.

Getting involved in talking shit about people, shows others that you're on their arsehole wavelength. And letting people get away with degrading you, show them that they can, so why would they ever stop.

While I'm probably quite good in a confrontation, it's something that happens very rarely in my life. Because I walk away. I realise something about the arsehole and decide not to be in their company any longer, so I leave. It can in fact look a bit random when it happens. I've put my cup down, coat on and left without a word before. I don't care what they think of me because as notes, I've already established they're an arsehole.

If you're not at Walking Away yet and want to make a stand my advice to you is only do this if you feel safe. Some arseholes are vicious bastards. I'm not so much recommending this, but rather hoping if you decide to make a stand that you stay strong and confident.

- Stand up in a strong stance.
- Maintain eye contact.
- Make sure your voice is loud, confident and that others can hear you.
- Even if/when they turn on you, recognise they are just scared wee kids who maybe didn't know any better.
- Know that they're now on unfamiliar territory – usually no one calls them out.

Chances are the next thing that happens is, they degrade you in some way and then they walk away. They are more clueless about this situation than you because you knew it was coming and got prepared. It's 100% taken them by shock. Now you've got your strong stance, here's a few things you could say…

- Speaking to someone like that is not okay!
- What the actual fuck?
- Why did you do/say that?

If you're in work…
- Can I see the 'Dignity at Work' policy because I'm pretty sure that's not okay?

Look at the victim of the arsehole and say:
- I'm really sorry (name) thought it was ok to just say/do that.
- You are such an arsehole! …and walk out!

The journey to standing against an arsehole could be a precarious one. I am sure though, that when you begin it will change your life. It will change the way you feel about yourself, the pride you feel as standing up for yourself or others will be great. I also believe that when we show others our bravery, they'll recognise it's possible for them too. They might be slow to follow, and you might never see it in action, but you'll change others when you show them it can be done.

Above all, when you stand against an arsehole, you make the world a better place. And the world is worth fighting for. Even if that 'world' is just your family, workplace, community group, neighbourhood, town, city or county. It will make a ripple that will be felt.

Challenge:
Call out the Arseholes at every opportunity!

CHAPTER 24
LET'S GET A BIT SCIENTIFIC: THE 'TIPPING POINT'

Definition

    Tipping Point

    noun.   *The time at which a change or an effect cannot be stopped.*

I've amazed myself that I have some science to back up my plan at this point! I've known about this science for a few years, and this book gifted me the chance to include it!

The facts here come from researchers at University of Pennsylvania, who in 2018 went out in a quest to find the Tipping Point for Large Scale Social Change.

Here's what *Science Magazine* had to say about it:

Tipping points in social convention

WHEN THE SIZE of a minority committed to social change reached just one-quarter of the group, it was consistently able to establish a new norm in the larger group, a finding with implications for behaviour in the workplace, online, and in our communities. When a minority group pushing change was below 25% of the total group, its efforts failed.

But when the committed minority reached 25%, there was an abrupt change in the group dynamic, and quickly a majority of the population adopted the new norm.

In one trial, a single person accounted for the difference between success and failure.

Science Magazine / 2018

If there is a tipping point when the minority can change the behaviour of the whole what does this mean for the arseholes in our lives?

Well, it means they're fucked. If 25% +1 of us grouping together and showing up differently in whatever grouping your thinking of, we can triumph!

Let's get some examples of what I mean:

Your Work Place

Let's try it on your team first. I get this could be anything from 3 to 300 people but if we start small maybe we'll get there quicker.

If you are a team of ten people or less, you only need two or three to get together and decide to banish arsehole behaviour to make this difference.

If you're a team of 50 you need 13 – but that's totally doable, I'm sure.

The key will always be to get the person who others listen to most as the first person on your team.

The first step must therefore always be – who is my first target and how do I get them?

Your Family

Well, perhaps a bit trickier but let's just find out if it's doable. To get to 25% it may be that you're the only one who needs to change their behaviour.

Now wouldn't that be interesting if, like Dorothy and the ruby slippers, you had the power all along?

Let's try it and see.

Perhaps you're not thinking about your own family in your home, but rather the extended family of parents, siblings, in-laws. In that case you'll need to work it like the workplace above.

Who is the most influential?

Your Friend Group

Like above, it depends on how big your group is, and how much you have invested in them.

My tendency towards truth talk would be to ask you – if your friend group is that bad why did you keep hanging around with them?

It's easier to walk away from friends than it is family and often workplaces. At some point we got okay with our friends being arseholes and forgot no one locked the door behind us.

The decision on whether to try or walk away is one only you can make.

Who knows, maybe it's one for after the experiment... I'll leave it with you.

The Great Arsehole Experiment! Where to Begin?

At the very start, of course!

My reckoning is that you have been identifying the main arseholes the whole way through this book. The Experiment is therefore a quest to see if we can 'kindness' the arsehole out of them, or if we can send them packing!

In case you hadn't realised those are our only two options if we're committed to changing our realities. Either they change or we move on without them. There's no halfway house in this stuff – you've seen them for the arseholes they are and now you can never see them any other way. Unless of course they show up in another way.

This is the beginning!

You've already started. The moment you picked up this book and decided to read it you set a change in motion. Of course, you could throw it in the bin, leave it on the train, stuff it down the back of the couch. But something has changed – even if that is simply the realisations you've had on this journey.

And you can't forget something you know to be true. You can pretend you've forgotten; continue being powerless; even say this book was a lot of shite.

But you know and I know that you have a choice to make at this point. Let it continue or be the change you've been waiting for!

STEP BY STEP GUIDE
1. Who is the Influencer of the group?

I'm not talking free eyelashes and invites to the opening of the new laundrette. The influencer can be quiet and unassuming. They might not even have an Insta page to show off said lashes. But you know that when they speak, others listen; when they laugh, others chuckle along and when anything is happening, they'll lead the dialogue on how it could best be dealt with.

They are the one look to and respect, even though they might not realise it.

Once you've identified this person, or if you're lucky to know who these people are Step 1 is complete!

2. How to get the 'influencer' onside?

You know them better than me.

Maybe it'll be a sausage roll at lunch time, an early morning start with them, or it will mean you need to go to lunch time yoga once a week.

Contemplate who they are and what your relationship with them is like.

Perhaps you are the influencer, or your best work pal is. In this case you've won a watch!

Once you have done Step 1 and Step 2, we're off and running to step 3...

3. Give them this book to read!

This book was always intended to be easy to read and if done in the one-go to take less than a couple of hours. You could have them on board by the end of their lunch break!

It does of course mean that your lucky influencer has someone to team up with in this experiment! But obvs, if you think of another who could join your ranks get back to step 1 and get them enlisted too.

4. Keep Repeating Until You Have 25% +1 person

There is no point in beginning the experiment if you only have 20%. It might not work, and you'll get down hearted and give up and the arseholes will have won!

You need to commit to the task at hand and to be on the safe side even get to 30% before you begin.

IMPORTANT POINT TO NOTE

I urge you to contemplate something at this point. Maybe the 25% tipping point has been working its magic in front of your eyes all along. Maybe its power could become crystal clear before you even begin.

Thinking of the group you're focussing on and contemplate how many really awful arseholes are in it? I concede it could feel like it's all of them.

But when you focus in, is it just a few who seem to influence everyone else. When they're on holidays, don't make it along to family occasions or miss a friends birthday party, does everyone else just have more fun? Are there less arguments? Are there fewer tears and dramas? Has this 25% rationale been hiding in plain sight all this time?

If you're eyes are widening and you're nodding, I hope this realisation gives you the push you need to get started! I mean it's not strictly speaking empirical evidence but it's as close as we'll get when talking about (metaphorical) arseholes!

Just for Fun!

> **Challenge:**
> Stop being an Arsehole every **Wednesday**, so you and those around you start to see how much better life can be when you make the decision to be a good guy.

If it feels like too much to make all the changes with all the arseholes at once I have an idea that feels like a fun way to begin. How about you commit to stopping the Arsehole Behaviour and standing up to it one day a week? I'm going to pick the day because that way we'll all be in it together and can start introducing our new way together. Even if we don't know each other we'll know that other people out there on the journey with you. Others, like you, who have had enough of the arseholes and want to move on in a world where these people are banished! The day I'm going for is Wednesday! I've always liked a Wednesday and always laughed when I hear people refer to it as 'hump' day!

If we decided that there would be none of this shite at the same time, I think a few things could happen…

- We'll be able to try out standing up to arseholes and indeed not being an arsehole ourselves. It'll be like a test drive of sorts.
- We'll get to see how life feels on a Wednesday as more people begin to get on board with us.
- Others will be lulled into what you're doing. If you're a woman, some arseholes will put the way you behaved

down to your hormones. But we'll know what's really happening, and we'll have a whole six days to work out how we'll deal with them by the time next Wednesday rolls around.

- Maybe as we get towards the 25% and as we recruit our team to help us, we'll start to see how much better things are. It'll be like test conditions that we can build upon.
- The more often you do it, the easier it will become. And the spaces between one Arsehole Free Wednesday and the next will get shorter, as we all begin to see that life is better on a Wednesday – but we're free to make the same change the other six days of the week too.
- When some things change so consistently, I really do believe that it will become like a big snowball rolling down a winter wonderland hill. It'll just keep going and growing and getting bigger and stronger and ultimately unable to stop, even if it wanted to.

CHAPTER 25
WE COULD CHANGE OUR WORLDS

Definition
    Change
        verb.   *To exchange one thing for another.*
                  To make or become different.

We Got Here! We're at the End!

The point of this book was to change lives. That sounds big and bold, and it might only serve the purpose of changing my own life. If so, it was worth every key tap.

I appreciate that it's a big claim to make and one that made me cringe many times before I dedicated it to these pages. But what better purpose can we really have other than wanting to change lives for the better?

When I first heard someone described as a 'Change Maker' I loved it, and instantly knew I wanted to be one. Yes, I could have shrunk to fit the piddly wee place other arseholes would like to see me in. Or I could rise into this exciting concept and make some moves to be a Change Maker! And that's what I decided to do by writing this book. And with every word I am urging you to come with me on this journey and be a Change Maker too. We only need 25% and we'll be there. Well, 25% plus one – and you don't know, maybe you're the 'one' we need to tip us over the edge and headfirst into social change.

In keeping it simple, I want to recap the most important points:

- Recognise what arsehole behaviours are?
- Make a mental note of where you see them played out in your life.
- Acknowledge who the Arseholes in your life are.
- Plot them on the Arsehole Map so you can work out what direction they're going in.
- Notice where you are on the Arsehole Map.
- Recognise you're not powerless to make a change.
- Know that we do all see arseholes – you're not alone and no it's not okay.
- Make a commitment to being a Change Maker in the areas of your life where you can.

Here's What I'm Hoping For...

I'm a very proud Glaswegian and consider myself lucky to have been born in my favourite city.

We are a people of almost 635,000 depending on where you draw the city lines.

I'm using this stat for these purposes.

Based on this figure I need 159,000 of my fellow Glasgow inhabitants to read this book or hear enough about it that they begin to join my ambition of ridding our streets of arseholes.

In a city where we could find ourselves with 159,000 people standing against all the stuff we've discussed in these pages, I believe we would change the direction of our dear green place, the lives of our people, the heights we could reach, the difference we could make, the way we would feel about everything.

In the crazy reality that I do get to this point, obviously with your help, I would do a few things…

1. I'd ask the police to tell me what the crime rate in Glasgow is on a Wednesday compared to other days of the week.
2. I'd request information from the NHS on how A&E admissions were on a Wednesday.
3. I'd ask the Education Department to report on behaviour in schools.
4. I'd ask supermarkets if customers were nicer.
5. I'd ask Traffic Wardens how many tickets they put on windscreens.

Basically, I would seek the opinion of everyone I could if they joined me on Wednesdays being their favourite day of the week, even though they didn't know why.

I'd ask one of the Universities in our city to start looking at and making much more sense of stats than I ever could. And then I'd show everyone, that when you recognise, you're an arsehole, and you stand against arsehole behaviour, that you can change a city and its inhabitants. That when a concerted minority come together in the name of good, that they can indeed change thousands of lives.

And once, I've shown this to the people of my city I'll have all I need to begin to change the world.

Thank you for coming on this journey with me. I think we might just be at the start of something really exciting. And if you're one of my fellow Glaswegians, remember when we were famous for our ships? Well, that's got nothing on being famous for showing others how to fundamentally change their way of being!

Arseholes!
Your time is up, and Glasgow is coming to get you!

ARSEHOLES: AN EPILOGUE

We reached the end of the book without mention of one of the biggest areas of our lives and worlds: our children and young people.

I was very intentional in not lumping them in with everyone else. Reason being that I believe our children and young people are magnificent. In fact, I believe they are our greatest hope for the future.

I won't say a word against them and would never include them in any of these chapters. Because to do so would be to blame them for all the shite their families, schools, communities, and society have been landing on them since the moment they entered the world.

If this book has had the impact that I intended, I imagine you could join me in the reflection that no wonder our young people act out. We fucked them up with our behaviours and it would be shameful to now blame them for it.

We finish this book down the rabbit hole of considering our own behaviours and how the effects of them have impacted our wider worlds. Wider as in society yes, but wider as in the people around us. The ones we love. The ones we made.

We all see the world from our own unique point of view. Work that I do with teams and coaching has shown me in recent years that while we assume everyone sees the stuff of life the way we do, we couldn't be further from the truth.

Others are not seeing what we see or feeling what we feel. We've all got a unique take on life. There are so many takes in fact that we can never really know how someone else sees it, reacts to it, or is affected by it.

When you add the fact that we're taking a unique perspective on the events we witness, the behaviour that surrounds us, and add in not understanding the world yet, or being full of a crazy amount of hormones, can we see how difficult it's been for our young people to get things right?

In fact, I could even argue that some of us have been showing our young people the exact behaviour time after time which such passion, that it was like a guide to being an arsehole! There, in their face every day. As they navigated all the stuff we navigate, they did it with a backdrop of being set some really bad examples by people who are older and apparently 'know how to adult'.

One of my best friends is a youth and community worker. I learn so much from her in how we should honour those we share our spaces with. I don't just mean our immediate spaces – I mean our towns and cities. What happens will have a ripple because everything does. If I don't care about how the group of teenage boys a mile away is being treated it will eventually be happening in my street too. We need to honour everyone and live lives that are worthy of the kind of society we want to be a part of.

During the pandemic something really fascinating happened. As we all know, there was a lot of vaccine hesitancy and the reasons for that were varied. But when it got linked to how people had experienced their lives it became clear that when society doesn't look after its children the impact will be felt for decades to come.

In the case of Vaccines to protect against Coronavirus, we knew and have now witnessed, that if enough of us didn't take the vaccine and make our spaces safer for everyone, that lock downs and isolation could remain part of our reality for many years to come. We needed a certain percentage of citizens to take one for the team. As I told anyone who would listen, the vaccine was never about the individual. It was always about the whole. I didn't get myself and my kids vaccinated just for us. I did it for my elderly neighbours, the people with cancer, those who had conditions that meant adding Covid to the mix would have led to their untimely demise.

I believe this is what happens when people stop trusting a society that has let them down.

Here is what was discovered when some people in Wales took a closer look...

Coronavirus vaccine hesitancy linked to childhood trauma

RESEARCH CONDUCTED BY Bangor University and Public Health Wales highlights the need for additional support to build trust in those affected by childhood trauma.

Reluctance or refusal to get vaccinated against Coronavirus infection (vaccine hesitancy), may be linked to the experience of traumatic events in childhood, such as neglect, domestic violence or substance misuse in the family home, suggests research funded by Public Health Wales and published in the BMJ Open.

Research conducted with adults in Wales identified that vaccine hesitancy was three times higher among people who had experienced four or more types of childhood trauma than it was among those who hadn't experienced any.

Childhood adversity has been shown to be linked to poorer mental well-being, with some studies suggesting it may lead to reduced trust in health and other public services. To explore this further, the research aimed to find out whether childhood trauma might be linked to levels of trust in NHS COVID-19 information; support for, and compliance with, Coronavirus restrictions (such as mandatory face coverings and social distancing); and intention to get vaccinated against the infection.

But the researchers point out that people who have experienced childhood trauma are "known to have greater health risks across the life-course. Results here suggest such individuals may have more difficulty with compliance with public health control measures and consequently require additional support." This is important not only for the current pandemic but for other future public health emergencies, they suggest.

"Understandably individuals who have suffered abuse, neglect or other forms of adversity as children may find it more difficult to develop trust in state systems provided for their protection and help. Here we have demonstrated how adults with a history of adverse childhood experiences are less likely to trust advice from health services and are subsequently less likely to either follow COVID-related restrictions or accept and act on information on the benefits of being vaccinated."

Professor Mark Bellis, Report author and Director of the World Health Organization Collaborating Centre at Public Health Wales, and Senior Research Fellow at Bangor University
Published by Bangor University / 4 February 2022

Childhood Trauma caused by those whose awful behaviours were never challenged influences us all. If we had protected those who were vaccine hesitant when they were children, maybe they would have taken the vaccine. But at some point, society showed them in, I'm sure, very traumatic ways, that we weren't going to look after them. So, when called upon to look after everyone else, they declined. And who can blame them?

Our children and young people need us to be better human beings than we often are. And at some point, in our future we may see the impact of not looking after them better or setting them a better example and making their places and spaces safer.

We allow the arseholes to continue at our own peril. I'm showing us one way we could make a change. It's not just about you when you stop being an arsehole.

It's about everyone, everywhere.

ACKNOWLEDGEMENTS

To my Siblings:
Helen, Margaret, Stephen
Thank you for doing life with me and being the first ones to encourage my rebellious nature. Knowing you are at my back has always been key to my bravery.

To My Friends:
Karen, Lewis, Lindsay, Mhairi, Paula & Sandra
When I walk through the world, I know I have you at my side. Your unfaltering support and love make me stand taller and braver in the world. Without your encouragement, I doubt this book would ever have been born.

To My Encourager & Book Launch Planner:
Emma, you got me excited about the book launch, which without a doubt pushed me through the final few months. Forever grateful for your friendship, belief, and encouragement. And of course, your event planning.

To My People:
I am humbled by all the good, brave, funny people I have in my life. Thank you for being here and being mostly okay with how much I swear, rant & ramble. It's because you laughed at my patter so often that I think I'm funny!

To My Place:
I have no doubt I was forged in the fire of my birthplace, a place I now belong to again. To the many friends I have here, to the spirit and resilience of its identity and for showing me life in all its extremes, I thank you. I will be forever in your debt, Govan.

To My Editor:
Graham – what a journey it's been. Thanks for sticking with me these last 30 years.

ABOUT THE AUTHOR

ANNE HUGHES is a motivational speaker, writer and broadcaster with more than 25 years' experience in public speaking and a depth of experience and knowledge in inspiring and motivating.

Having encountered a life-changing episode in 2017, facing death and enduring a lengthy recovery, Anne is now driven to encourage people to act immediately to ensure their lives feel better on the inside.

Anne produces and hosts two podcasts, has produced, and hosted over 150 interview format shows for Sunny Govan Radio and is a regular contributor to BBC Radio Scotland. She has appeared in three series of *The People's News* on BBC Scotland TV; written more than 100 columns for *Glasgow Live* and was a contributing author to the book *She's Unstoppable*, published in August 2020.

In June 2024, Anne releases her own take on self-help books with *People Are Arseholes*, written with the intention of making her city and country a kinder place to live.

Anne lives in Glasgow with her husband and three children.

www.annehughesignite.co.uk

If this book does what it's intended to do, watch out for the sequel...

www.ingramcontent.com/pod-product-compliance
Lightning Source LLC
Chambersburg PA
CBHW070426010526
44118CB00014B/1918